BECKETT / BECKETT

A Truth in art is that whose contradictory is also true.

OSCAR WILDE

BECKETT/BECKETT

VIVIAN MERCIER

SOUVENIR PRESS

To Eilís

PROLOGUE
(Spoken by the Author in his Own Person)

The second New York production of *Waiting for Godot*,
imported from Los Angeles, had an all-black cast: an early
proof of the universality of the play. On Friday nights during the run, the theater was turned into a seminar room
after the final curtain. A panel of "experts" — a psycho-
analyst, an actor, an English professor, and so on — sat on-
stage and conducted a dialogue with those in the auditorium;
admission was free. The night I attended this symposium,
the most effective contribution was made by a member of
the audience who asked the panel the rhetorical question,
"Isn't *Waiting for Godot* a sort of living Rorschach [ink-
blot] test?" He was clapped and cheered by most of those
present, who clearly felt as I still do that most interpreta-
tions of that play — indeed of Samuel Beckett's work as a
whole — reveal more about the psyches of the people who
offer them than about the work itself or the psyche of its
author.

To this rule, if it is one, I don't profess to be an excep-

tion: on the contrary, the book that follows will be seen to
offer a rather personal view of its subject — though not, I
hope, a wildly idiosyncratic one. Not that I can claim any
special intimacy with Beckett the·man: I have met him
only three times and, out of respect for his privacy, made
very few notes after these meetings. I have also received
about a dozen letters from him, one or two of which might
be described as self-revelatory, but I have quoted only passages that are factual and neutral in tone, and very few even
of those.

What makes my view of Beckett personal is chiefly the
fact that, having attended the same boarding-school and
university as he did, I was constantly aware of him as someone not very much older than myself (thirteen years), from
the same rather philistine Irish Protestant background, who
had become the sort of avant-garde artist and critic that I
longed to be.

A brief chronicle of this long-distance relationship with
Beckett may not be entirely without interest. Born in April
1919, I entered Portora Royal School, Enniskillen, in Sep-
tember 1928, just over five years after Beckett's departure.
It was not until 1934, however, that I first heard of him;
the news must have made a great impression, for I have
kept its source ever since — a leaflet entitled "Old Portora
Union: Terminal Letter No. 35." The then Headmaster,
Rev. E. G. Seale, distributed his "letter" (dated July 1934)
to all present members of the school as well as "old boys."
Having mentioned a book by another alumnus, J. Chartres
Molony, Seale continued:

> But Old Portorans seem to be going strong in the lit-
> erary world. S. B. Becket [sic] has now brought out a vol-

ume entitled "More Pricks than Kicks." It is described as "A piece of literature memorable, exceptional, the utterance of a very modern voice." The *Spectator* devoted a column of criticism, mostly favourable, to this book. We must heartily congratulate its author on such a reception to his first work of fiction. His "Proust" was published a couple of years earlier.

Although Enniskillen is in Northern Ireland, so that the subsequent banning of *More Pricks than Kicks* in the Irish Free State had no legal effect there, I noticed that the book did not turn up in the school library: Portora in those years was just beginning to admit that it had been the alma mater of Oscar Wilde and wanted no fresh notoriety. All I could do was to look up the *Spectator* review and try to discover what this strangely named book was about. (Any Portora boy of that vintage would have recognized, as I did, the allusion to the conversion of St. Paul: in the King James Bible, the voice from Heaven says, "It is hard for thee to kick against the pricks.") I also identified Beckett, wrongly, as the captain in an old photograph of a cricket first eleven. Our senior French master, S. B. Wynburne, had been an exact contemporary and close academic rival of Beckett at Trinity College, Dublin.

I myself entered Trinity in 1936 at the same age as Beckett had done and was accepted by the same tutor, Dr. A. A. Luce. Like Beckett, I read Honors French with Professor T. B. Rudmose-Brown; my other Honors subject was English, which Beckett had also read for a time before giving it up to concentrate on Italian. Facts like these explain the emphasis on Beckett as a member of a particular social class and ethnic grouping, with a particular type of education, especially in Chapters 2, 3 and 4 below. Beckett is unique, as we all are, but he has not descended from another planet. Irvin Ehrenpreis, in his exemplary life of Swift, anxious like me to present his subject as neither a deity nor a monster, has drawn a number of parallels between the future Dean and his contemporaries, including of course some of his fellow-undergraduates.

After the Trinity B.A., Beckett's and my paths in life soon diverged sharply, but I remained constantly aware of him. In 1938, while still an undergraduate, I read Kate O'Brien's enthusiastic review of *Murphy*; when she mentioned the novel again later in the year, I decided to spend a quarter of my weekly allowance on the single copy of it that had languished on Hodges Figgis's shelves for several months. I fell in love with the book at once and reread it every year until it was lost or stolen about 1945. By then I had also read *Proust*, the essay on Joyce's *Work in Progress*, and, under the watchful eye of a Trinity librarian, the banned *More Pricks than Kicks*. Quite possibly my Ph.D. thesis, for which I received a Trinity doctorate in December 1945, was the first to pay serious attention, however briefly, to Beckett's fiction. I had already praised *Murphy* in print, in the January-March 1943 issue of the *Dublin Magazine*, while reviewing Eric Cross's *The Tailor and Ansty*:

> . . . Irish literature for the past twenty years has remained in the backwater of dialect *reportage*. Joyce at least mingled imagination with his realism, but his successors have largely ignored the fantastic side of *Ulysses*. Only during the last three or four years have two books appeared which contain both Joyce's ingredients—Sam-

uel Beckett's *Murphy* and Flann O'Brien's *At Swim-Two-Birds*. Both these books have been undeservedly neglected in favour of others more obviously in the "oral tradition."

(Evidently I was already losing patience with the topic of my doctoral thesis, "Realism in Anglo-Irish Fiction 1916-1940.") I praised the same novels again at greater length in a "Letter from Ireland" published in Cyril Connolly's *Horizon* (April 1946); there is reason to believe that Beckett saw the mention and was grateful for it. The substance of the *Horizon* comments appeared yet again in "Dublin Under the Joyces," my contribution to a symposium edited by Seon Givens, *James Joyce: Two Decades of Criticism* (New York, 1948). Beckett may not have seen this essay, but another contributor to the symposium, Hugh Kenner, had his attention directed to Beckett by it: for this and other reasons he dedicated his first book on Beckett to me.

Although constantly on the alert for new work by Beckett after World War II, I found nothing except his French translation of *Murphy* (1947). After trying to persuade one or two New York publishers to reprint the original English, I prepared excerpts from *Murphy* for inclusion in what has since become a standard anthology in the United States, 1000 *Years of Irish Prose: Part I, The Literary Revival.* Unfortunately, I was overruled by my co-editor and the publisher: our Beckett-less anthology appeared in 1952, a few months before *En attendant Godot* had its first performance. By the end of 1953, I owned copies of that play, the three volumes of the trilogy in French and, I think, *Watt.*

During the years 1953-60, work on *The Irish Comic Tradition* — a book which frequently mentions Beckett — filled so much of my time that the late Stanley Edgar Hyman, never one to mince words, expressed surprise at my failure to "cash in on Beckett." Nevertheless, I did write several short articles and reviews, some of which I have felt tempted to reprint in an appendix to the present work, if only as a reminder that in the 1950's I adopted, and in at least one case initiated, some of the standard critical attitudes to Beckett. For instance, a long notice of the first American edition of *Waiting for Godot* in *Hudson Review* (Winter 1955) stressed Beckett's Irishness and his comic techniques, as did a *Commonweal* review of the first American printing of *Murphy* and other items (17 May 1957). In the *New Republic* (19 September 1955), my review of *Molloy* appeared under the title "Beckett and the Search for Self," anticipating later and longer studies with similar titles. "The Mathematical Limit," a review of *The Unnamable* in *The Nation* (14 February 1959), appears to have been the first attempt to define Beckett's use of mathematics — irrational numbers, series, permutations and combinations, perhaps analytical geometry — in his novels; Kenner later devoted a chapter to this in his first book on Beckett. Nothing else I have written on Beckett has attracted so much notice as this 1800-word article, except one phrase in an *Irish Times* review of the Faber first printing of *Waiting for Godot:* "a play in which nothing happens, *twice.*"

The last paragraph is perhaps more interesting to its author than to his readers, but it frees me of the need to discuss any of these topics in the present book unless I have something new to say about them. *Beckett / Beckett* is intended to be a "second-generation" contribution to the study of its subject, as different as possible from the book I

might have written fifteen years ago. Why I never wrote
that book could be partly guessed by anyone who read the
last of my 1950's reviews, "How to read *Endgame*," in the
Griffin for June 1959: clearly I disliked that play. I still do,
but it was events in my personal life rather than distaste for
a particular work of his that impelled me to shun Beckett:
at the end of 1959, the mysterious disease that had temporarily paralyzed my wife in 1958 and temporarily blinded
her the next year was diagnosed as multiple sclerosis. It
may seem paradoxical that this confirmation of Beckett's
gloomy estimate of the human condition should have
turned me against his work, but I wrote virtually nothing
more on him until after Gina's death in 1971.

So much for autobiography, then. The structure of this
book is explained in Chapter 1, but something needs to be
said here about the fewness of notes and the absence of
bibliography. No page references are given for quotations
from Beckett's works, except when these come from uncollected material in periodicals or symposia, or — in two
places only — where it is not otherwise clear that Beckett
is being quoted. Most of his works are short, so that passages from them are fairly easily located; also, *Murphy* is
divided into chapters, *Watt* and *How It Is* into parts. Only
in the trilogy do real difficulties arise; but these, for readers
of English, appear insoluble, at least for the time being.
There are three English-language editions of *Three Novels*,
each with different pagination, as well as two or three editions of each of the separate novels — *Molloy, Malone Dies,
The Unnamable* — each again with its own pagination.
Beckett novices will presumably take my quotations on
trust; hardened Becketteers, who know how easy it is to

distort a passage by depriving it of its context, will also know where that context is to be found. I might have arbitrarily decided to use the Grove Press *Collected Edition*, but it lays no claim to textual accuracy and is not readily available outside the United States and Canada. At times I have quoted from the French texts, either to illustrate Beckett's French style or to point out differences between the French and English versions; for the sake of consistency, page references are not given for these passages either. Let me add that I have read through at least once in French every work of Beckett's originally written in that language.

More or less complete check-lists of Beckett's publications are supplied in many other studies of his work: Ruby Cohn's *Back to Beckett* sets out their chronology with a neatness that could hardly be surpassed. As for the ever-rising flood of books and articles about Beckett, I have read few of them and found even fewer to be of use for my purposes. Those that I have quoted are fully documented in my notes: I am deeply grateful to their authors. Paradoxically, my greatest debt is owed to a book not yet published as this one goes to press: Deirdre Bair's biography of Samuel Beckett. Far more important than the facts about his earlier life for which I have thanked Mrs. Bair in the notes is the sense of his total personality that a reading of her typescript draft gave me: this has undoubtedly influenced my interpretation of his work in many places, sometimes perhaps in ways of which I am not fully aware.

Thanks to a fellowship from the John Simon Guggenheim Foundation, I was able to do some of the research for this book in France and Ireland and to begin writing it in Dublin. The Committee on Research and Creative Work of the University of Colorado also gave great assistance by awarding me a Faculty Fellowship for the academic year 1972-73. I thank the Academic Senate at the University of California, Santa Barbara, for a Faculty Research Grant and the English Department for generous clerical assistance.

I offer my warm personal thanks to the following: Mr. Beckett, first of all, for unfailing kindness and patience over the past twenty years, and for permission to use all quotations from his letters and uncollected prose in English and French and to translate literally from his works in French wherever necessary; Wallace Fowlie, Hal Kelling, Hugh Kenner and Frank Kermode for their sponsorship; Kay Hudson for her meticulous typing; James Raimes, Stephanie Golden, Catharine Carver and others at Oxford University Press for editorial assistance; Catherine Linnet for the initial suggestion; David Bolt, Georges Borchardt and Rosemary Macomber for indispensable help; John Calder, Peter du Sautoy, Jérôme Lindon and Barney Rosset for help with permissions; and Rachel Burrows for excerpts from her notebook.

Parts of Chapter 4 represent a revised version of an article entitled "Unity of Inaction: Beckett and Racine," which appeared in *The Nation* for 31 August 1974. An earlier version of Chapter 2 was published in *Yeats, Joyce, and Beckett*, edited by Kathleen McGrory and John Unterecker (Lewisburg, Pa.: Bucknell University Press, 1976).

Santa Barbara, California   V.M.
Thanksgiving 1976

CONTENTS

BECKETT / BECKETT

1

THESIS / ANTITHESIS

"A Truth in art is that whose contradictory is also true."[1] One could hardly find a pithier statement of my approach to Samuel Beckett than this sentence from the concluding paragraph of "The Truth of Masks." Despite the title of Wilde's essay, I had no intention when I first chose this epigraph of invoking Yeats's theory that the mask or anti-self is the source of every true artist's best work. Yet all I know of Beckett the man suggests that he is gentle, compassionate, tolerant and serious — whereas Beckett the artist is often cruel, pitiless, intolerant and ribald. To quote Yeats, "The work is the man's flight from his entire horoscope. . . ."[2] Beckett, however, would not agree that if this be true his work is any the better for it. Like "Hic" in Yeats's dialogue-poem "Ego Dominus Tuus," he might well affirm "And I would find myself and not an image," rejecting the doctrine of the anti-self put forward by Yeats's spokesman, "Ille." In his 1934 article "Recent Irish Poetry," Beckett rebuked Yeats and all his school for their "flight from self-

3

awareness"; he accused them of abandoning "the centre" for "the circumference," which is "an iridescence of themes . . . segment after segment of cut-and-dried sanctity and loveliness."[3] (Note his malicious quotation from Yeats's then-recent lines: "We were the last romantics — chose for theme / Traditional sanctity and loveliness. . . ."[4])

For Beckett, art must always be founded upon "self-awareness" or, in the phrase he later preferred, "self-perception." The only thing outside the self that the artist can hope to express is — in the words of the 1934 article — "the space that intervenes between him and the world of objects." Before he can do even this, of course, he must go in quest of the self and strive to perceive it clearly — an awesome task. As Beckett told John Gruen in an interview more than thirty years after his 1934 *prise de position*, ". . . self-perception is the most frightening of all human observations . . . when man faces himself he is looking into the abyss."[5] In *Proust* (1931), however, he had already insisted that there was no other path open to the serious artist:

> The only fertile research is excavatory, immersive, a contraction of the spirit, a descent. The artist is active, but negatively, shrinking from the nullity of extra-circumferential phenomena, drawn in to the core of the eddy. He cannot practise friendship, because friendship is the centrifugal force of self-fear, self-negation. . . . We are alone. We cannot know and we cannot be known.

To some extent, Beckett is here paraphrasing Proust, but he writes with such eloquence that it is hard to believe he is not already expressing his own conviction — one that he was to reiterate in his 1934 article and on so many later occasions.

There is all the difference in the world, however, between holding a conviction and putting it into practice. It was not until Beckett started to write in French, at some point in the year 1945, that the total immersion in self, the descent into the core of the eddy, finally took place. I am tempted to posit a conscious change of direction on Beckett's part, closely resembling the experience so tantalizingly hinted at in *Krapp's Last Tape*. Krapp is listening to a tape he made to record the chief events of his thirty-ninth year:

> Spiritually a year of profound gloom and indigence until that memorable night in March, at the end of the jetty, in the howling wind, never to be forgotten, when suddenly I saw the whole thing. The vision, at last. This I fancy is what I have chiefly to record this evening, against the day when my work will be done and perhaps no place left in my memory, warm or cold, for the miracle that . . . (*hesitates*) . . . for the fire that set it alight. What I suddenly saw then was this, that the belief I had been going on all my life, namely — (*Krapp switches off impatiently, winds tape forward, switches on again*) — great granite rocks the foam flying up in the light of the lighthouse and the wind-gauge spinning like a propellor, clear to me at last that the dark I have always struggled to keep under is in reality my most — (*Krapp curses, switches off, winds tape forward, switches on again*) — unshatterable association until my dissolution of storm and night with the light of the understanding and the fire. . . .

At this point Krapp switches off the machine once again and finally winds the tape far enough ahead to reach a love-scene, which he finds far more interesting at his present age

of sixty-nine. The fragments of the storm-scene that we
have been vouchsafed, however, seem of the greatest relevance to Beckett's own life in his thirty-ninth year. (13
April 1945 was his thirty-ninth birthday.) The dark that
Krapp has always struggled to keep under is, one may guess,
in reality his most valuable subject-matter and, in a paradoxical way, his greatest source of enlightenment.* He has
established an unshatterable mental association, which will
persist until his death, between storm and night on the one
hand and the light of understanding on the other. Krapp,
who no doubt had hitherto believed in the supreme significance and value of the daylight world, learned to appreciate
the night world, the dark depths of the sea, and the dark
within himself. As the sixth chapter of *Murphy* demonstrates (by describing the three zones of Murphy's mind:
light, half-light, and dark), Krapp was not the first Beckett
character to develop this appreciation. But whereas Beckett
had described Murphy's mind from the outside, in the series of French works begun in 1945 he plunged deeper and
deeper within the dark of his own self. *L'Innommable* (*The
Unnamable*) marked the farthest he could go in this direction; in that novel, as he told Israel Shenker in 1956,

> ". . . there's complete disintegration. No 'I,' no 'have,'
> no 'being.' No nominative, no accusative, no verb.
> There's no way to go on.
> "The very last thing I wrote — 'Textes pour Rien' —
> was an attempt to get out of the attitude of disintegra-
> tion, but it failed."[6]

This interview appeared in the *New York Times* on 6 May
1956; not many days later I received a note from Beckett

* Compare "the dark that enlightens the spirit." (See below, p. 102.)

postmarked 16 May which read, in part: "Up to my navel in sudden work so forgive more now." By the end of the year he had finished *Fin de partie* (*Endgame*), the grimmest of his plays but also the one in which he felt he had most nearly achieved what he set out to do. Furthermore, he had written a radio play in English "to come out of the dark" — *All That Fall.*

The dark has many connotations for Beckett. Some of them have been dealt with by James Knowlson, who writes of "the key images of light and dark, heat and cold, mind and mindlessness, being and non-being, that have recurred throughout Beckett's work. . . ."[7] Mindlessness and non-being are certainly important equivalents for the dark, but the second of the two pages that Knowlson reproduces in facsimile from Beckett's manuscript notebook, "written for his own production of *Krapp's Last Tape* at the Schiller-Theater Werkstatt, Berlin, October 5th, 1969," offers some further equivalents of the greatest interest:

> Note that Krapp decrees physical (ethical) incompatibility of light (spiritual) and dark (sensual) only when he intuits possibility of their reconciliation intellectually as rational-irrational. He turns from fact of anti-mind alien to mind to thought of anti-mind constituent of mind. He is thus ethically correct (Signaculum sinus) through intellectual transgression, the duty of reason being not to join but to separate (deliverance of imprisoned light). For this sin he is punished as shown by the aeons.

> Note that if the giving of the black ball to the white dog represents the sacrifice of sense to spirit the form here too is that of a mingling.[8]

As the first page reproduced by Knowlson clarifies, Beckett is here playing with Gnostic dualism. I find it hard to believe that Beckett habitually equates the dark with the sensual; for Murphy, for example, his own private dark is more akin to the spiritual: it is the daylight world that is the domain of the senses. The association of the irrational, of "anti-mind constituent of mind," with the dark is much more illuminating, so to speak. Also associated with the dark in Beckett's mind, I believe, are ignorance and impotence. As he remarked to Israel Shenker in the interview already quoted, "I think anyone nowadays, who pays the slightest attention to his own experience finds it the experience of a non-knower, a non-can-er." In the same interview, comparing his own work to that of James Joyce, Beckett said:

> "With Joyce the difference is that Joyce was a superb manipulator of material — perhaps the greatest. He was making words do the absolute maximum of work. There isn't a syllable that's superfluous. The kind of work I do is one in which I'm not master of my material. The more Joyce knew the more he could. He's tending toward omniscience and omnipotence as an artist. I'm working with impotence, ignorance. I don't think impotence has been exploited in the past."[9]

Beckett had in fact begun his career by trying to imitate Joyce's omniscience and omnipotence. "Sedendo et Quiescendo" and much of *More Pricks Than Kicks* were pastiches of Joyce's *Work in Progress* (later to become *Finnegans Wake*) and therefore crammed with esoteric allusions, learned innuendoes and polyglot puns. *Murphy* is only slightly more sparing with these, and its "omniscient" narrator shows awareness of his omnipotence too in asides like this one: "All the puppets in this book whinge sooner or later, except Murphy, who is not a puppet." Or this: "The above passage is carefully calculated to deprave the cultivated reader." *Watt* was the first of Beckett's books to explore ignorance and impotence, but it still suffered from the presence of an "omniscient" narrator, as did *Mercier et Camier*. The adoption of a first-person narrator in the trilogy solved that problem very simply.

As I have already noted, this phase of Beckett's creativity stretches from 1945 to about May 1956. When the Shenker interview was published, it was already out of date. The dark continues to manifest itself in Beckett's later work — often quite literally, as in the lighting directions for *Krapp's Last Tape* and *Play* — but the impotence and ignorance of the author become harder and harder to believe in. *Comment c'est* (1960; *How It Is*), the last major work to be composed originally in French, has a protagonist who crawls and murmurs in the mud, the very personification, it would seem, of impotence and ignorance. Yet he engages in complicated mathematical speculations and finally explodes his whole predicament as illusory by sheer effort of mind. Furthermore, it would be ridiculous for the Beckett of *Comment c'est* to claim any longer that he was not master of his material. For this novel (poem?) he created a new style, of telegraphic conciseness: brief phrases linked together in unpunctuated paragraphs (stanzas?), each with its own cadence. As for the plays in English written before and after this French work, at least two of them, *Krapp's Last Tape* (1958) and *Play* (1962), could almost be described as "slick" because of the economy and precision with which they make their points. *Happy Days* (1961), though more open-ended, has proved conventional enough to attract the reigning ladies of the theater. We can quote in praise of Beckett the very words that he used to glorify Joyce: "He was making words do the absolute maximum of work. There isn't a syllable that's superfluous." The later works of fiction known as *Residua* deserve similar praise, being full of implications despite their brevity. Beckett told Brian Finney that "they are residual (1) Severally, even when that does not appear of which each is all that remains and (2) In relation to whole body of previous work."[10] He may therefore claim not to be master of his material in that he is unable to produce complete works, but no one would ever have suspected that *Le Dépeupleur* (*The Lost Ones*) was incomplete if Beckett had not suggested the possibility. Apparently the fifteenth and final section of the work was added just before its French publication in 1970: "Sections 1-14 of *Le Dépeupleur*, Beckett writes, were at the time 'abandoned because of its complexity getting beyond control.' "[11] Nevertheless, thanks to this last-minute addition, the fifteen sections read like a complete and satisfying whole.

This movement in Beckett's career from omniscience to nescience, rationality to irrationality, omnipotence to impotence, light to darkness, and then back again recalls the quotation from Wilde with which I began. In reviewing the entire work of a writer of genius, the critic has no right to say, "He is this and not that," even where *this* and *that* are polar opposites. There is always, I believe, a dialectic at work in the minds of the greatest writers: perhaps their greatness consists precisely in the power to hold two equal

and opposite ideas in the mind at once. David H. Hesla has
written a whole book — an excellent one — to prove that
"the shape of Beckett's art is the shape of dialectic."[12] Each
of the major works is, in Hesla's opinion,

> a synthesis of the positive and the negative, the comic
> and the "pathetic," the yes and the no. . . . Optimism
> and pessimism, hope and despair, comedy and tragedy
> are counterbalanced by one another: none of them is
> allowed to become an Absolute.[13]

Unfortunately, despite Beckett's own insistence that "the
key word in my play is 'perhaps,' "[14] too many of his critics
continue to seek an absolute and even to proclaim that they
have found one.

The aim of the chapters that follow, as their titles imply,
is to focus attention on certain aspects of this all-pervasive
dialectic. They do this, I hope, in three different ways. First
of all, the chapters entitled "Ireland / The World" and
"Artist / Philosopher" deal with areas in which critics have
by now agreed that a dialectic is present: I myself was one
of the first to stress Beckett's Irishness, while John Fletcher's *Samuel Beckett's Art* inaugurated a fresh critical emphasis implicit in its title. Familiar though these topics may
have become, I nevertheless feel that I have something
partly new to say, especially on the first. At least three
other chapters — "Gentleman / Tramp," "Classicism / Absurdism," "Eye / Ear" — were written in the belief that
Beckett criticism, while somewhat aware of each dialectic,
tends to emphasize one of its poles to the almost total neglect of the other. In the chapter headings, to dramatize this
neglect, I have put what might be considered the antithesis
before the too-familiar thesis. The chapter "Painting / Mu-

sic" falls into yet a third category, being concerned with a dialectic that, so far as I can discover, Beckett criticism has not previously recognized. Finally, to which of my three categories should I assign "Woman / Man"? Can it really be possible that the critics have failed to locate in Beckett's work what constituted Yeats's favorite example of an antinomy? If not, they have certainly neglected it.

Once adopted, this dialectical approach to Beckett can become dangerously attractive: possible chapter headings proliferate almost to infinity. Furthermore, a book organized in this way offers an easy gambit to a dyspeptic reviewer: "Why hasn't the author given us a chapter on . . . ?" One answer to such quibbling can be found in the law of diminishing returns. For example, the opposition compassion / cruelty seems an ideal instrument for the dissection of Beckett, but the opposition woman / man — at least as understood here — subsumes it. Another opposition subsumed by woman / man is optimism / pessimism or — as Hesla alternatively phrases it — hope / despair. It may not be true that all Beckett's women characters hope and all his men despair, but it is less blatantly untrue than the converse.

A reader might ask with more justification why someone who has written as often as I have about the comic aspects of Beckett's work should omit the seemingly inevitable opposition between comic and tragic. But where in fact is the tragic to be found? Beckett cannot believe in, or at least cannot create, a genuine tragic hero — powerful, proud, yet essentially good save for the tragic flaw. Beckett's antiheroes do not aspire, so they can never fall. Much of the mirthless laughter they elicit from us springs precisely from this lack of aspiration: they expect so little from life, and yet their minimal expectations are frustrated. For instance, in *En attendant Godot* Vladimir says, "Ce soir on couchera peut-être chez lui [Godot], au chaud, au sec, le ventre plein, sur la paille." It does not seem too much to hope for: to sleep on straw at Godot's house, warm, dry, and with a full belly; yet of course it never happens. In the English-language editions, Vladimir does not even hope for such ordinary material comforts: this speech has been omitted.

Another deterrent to tragedy is the absence of free will from Beckett's world: very early in his career, his characters become slaves to Fate. Murphy still possesses free will but is anxious to surrender it to his horoscope; Watt is neither free to go when it is time to stay, nor free to stay when it is time to go. The same is true of Molloy, Moran, Malone and the Unnamable. Mercier and Camier have some freedom, but their journey is as compulsive and unmotivated as that of the protagonist of *How It Is*. Didi and Gogo suggest that they are free to wait for Godot or not, as they please, but in fact they cannot leave the immediate vicinity of the stage: their predicament is summed up at the end of each act when one of them says "Let's go," but they do not move. Hamm and Clov similarly believe that they "hesitate . . . to end" but in fact seem incapable of ending. In later plays, a whistle, a goad, a bell and a spotlight elicit tropistic behavior from one or all of the characters. Beckett, who believes in so little, appears to take this oppressive force for granted: perhaps it is often no more than life itself, which compels us to leave the womb and journey toward the tomb. Suicide, the supreme act of free will, seems beyond the capacity of Beckett's protagonists; only minor characters here and there succeed in it. The ultimate rebellion in Beckett's world is not to end one's existence but to deny it: as Mouth does in *Not I*, as the Unnamable does, as the narrator does at the end of *How It Is*. Let us note too, without attempting to explain it, that the characters in the radio plays seem to have more freedom — though Henry in *Embers* is not at liberty to stop talking.

We may concede that *Endgame* comes closer to being a tragedy than any of the other works; yet the death of Nell — if she does die — evokes only pity: she has made no visible struggle against her fate. Like Dickens's Little Nell, her end is pathetic not tragic. Hamm and Clov, whose deaths seem imminent though they have not yet occurred at the play's end, are grotesque rather than tragic. In their cruelty to each other and to Nagg and Nell, they reveal themselves as monsters rather than men. We can laugh at them for their ugliness of body and mind, we can fear them, but we cannot pity them nor identify with them.

It seemed inevitable at one time that a chapter bearing some such title as "Speech / Silence" or "Moreness / Lessness" would form part of this book: Beckett is at once the most garrulous and the most laconic of living writers. Although *The Unnamable* is much shorter than most contemporary novels in English, one cannot open it at random and read a page or two without feeling caught up in an interminable flow. The book stops but does not end, for the protagonist's last words are "I'll go on." On the other hand, no articulate sounds at all are uttered in *Breath*, the two *Acts Without Words*, or *Film*. All Beckett's new work since 1965 has been of minimal length, yet, because of the reluctance to end already noted, one cannot say that it attains silence. On the contrary, Mouth in *Not I* seems ready to talk for ever: her voice is audible though not intelligible before the curtain rises and continues, unintelligible, after the curtain falls. *Sans* (1969), translated as *Lessness* (1970), does not quite live up to its name in either language. The first half of this work consists of sixty "sentences," many without a main verb; in the second half, each of these sentences is repeated once, their order being determined by an aleatory process. The sentences can, however, be rearranged to form six groups or categories, each with a common subject-matter, of ten sentences apiece. Hardly a formula for creating a comprehensive work of literature, one might think. Beckett, however, has divulged the subjects of all six categories: the fifth, "a denial of past and future," and the sixth, "an affirmation of past and future,"[15] together make up another version of the opposition being / non-being. Thus the work, though so short, is once again open-ended: of the ten sentences in the sixth category, one at least holds out no promise of ultimate silence: "He will curse God again as in the blessed days face to the open sky the passing deluge."

I once suggested, in a review of *The Unnamable*, that Beckett had established "content zero, length infinity," as the limits of the novel form. In some recent short works he seems to have interchanged the axes to make content infinity, length zero, the limits within which he now operates. Earlier, *Play* with its stage direction *"Repeat play exactly"* had established the concept of a small number of speeches and actions repeatable to infinity. Even before that, there was Vladimir's circular song about the dog in *Waiting for Godot*.* The inherent paradox of a finite number of possibilities repeated to infinity appeals to Beckett, as his frequent use of mathematical permutations and combinations in *Murphy* and *Watt* suggests: it is surely one of his master-metaphors for life. Though Beckett has often quoted Democritus' aphorism "Nothing is more real than nothing," and has said and written — especially in *The Unnamable* — a great deal about the virtues of silence, his work eludes the categories set up by books like Ihab Hassan's *The Literature of Silence* and Claude Mauriac's *L'Alittérature contemporaine*. He is not — in this life at least — going to reach either silence or nothingness. If he were, the neglect of his early work through nearly two decades would have supplied ample inducement for him to fall silent long ago. There is of course a dialectic in his work between silence and garrulity, but the subject has been done more than justice by previous critical studies.

Oddly enough, the life / death opposition has not been dealt with as thoroughly. Life of course is deadly in the Beckett world, but in fact he has not written much about death itself — merely a series of "friendly undertaker" jokes concerning its pleasures. He is no good at death scenes, except in the sense that most of his scenes from life are living-death scenes. He can produce nothing more memorable for the moment of death than Malone's "gurgles of outflow," while his account of life after death is necessarily almost indistinguishable from his account of life before it.

The dialectic infinity / entropy possesses more interest, perhaps, since it concerns the fate of the universe as well as

* See below, p. 86.

the individual. Beckett has long been familiar with the concept of entropy: one might say that if the Second Law of Thermodynamics did not exist, he would have found it necessary to invent it. As early as 1934, in "Recent Irish Poetry," he jeered at "the thermolaters — and they pullulate in Ireland — adoring the stuff of song as incorruptible, uninjurable and unchangeable. . . ."[16] Presumably he meant by "thermolaters" ("heat-worshippers") those who do not believe in or have never heard of entropy. In *The Lost Ones* (1972), translated from *Le Dépeupleur* (1970), he presents what seems to be a model of an entropic social system: "Abode where lost bodies roam each searching for its lost one. . . . One body per square metre or two hundred bodies in all round numbers." These bodies (human ones, it emerges) are confined in a cylinder "fifty metres round and eighteen high"; they behave according to certain inner compulsions and certain external though unwritten laws. Although entropy seems at last to supervene, the opening sentence of the final paragraph is highly ambiguous:

> So on infinitely until towards the unthinkable end if this notion is maintained a last body of all by feeble fits and starts is searching still.

If the process continues "infinitely," how can there be an "end," even an "unthinkable" one? Infinity itself, perhaps, is finite insofar as it leads to entropy. Though Beckett believes in the ultimate exhaustion of all the available energy in the universe, he knows that this will not happen in our time.

The phrases "in our time" and "of our time" will be

found infrequently, if at all, in the chapters that follow. It is hard for one who like myself has been reading Beckett for nearly forty years to summon up the kind of enthusiasm for his modernity or "post-modernity" that was felt by French critics in the 1950's or American critics in the 1960's. Beckett's doubts about the goodness of human nature or the grandeur of human destiny may have seemed very timely in those decades, or indeed in the 1930's, when I began to read him. He himself, however, has always been the first to remind us — with quotations from Job and Democritus, from Dante, Schopenhauer and Leopardi, and most recently with notebook entries about Gnosticism — that his attitudes are as old as literature itself.

It still seems premature to attempt a chapter based on the opposition for an age / for all time, although Beckett's preference for what he has called "fundamental sounds" might appear likely to guarantee the permanence of *The Unnamable* or *Waiting for Godot*, *Murphy* or *Endgame*, *Malone Dies* or *Happy Days*. Posterity, though, plays the oddest tricks. Look at the reputation of one of Beckett's favorite English writers, Dr. Samuel Johnson. *Rasselas*, *London*, *The Vanity of Human Wishes*, all make fundamental sounds of a truly Beckettian pessimism; they are the works on which Johnson's fame as a creative artist depends. Most non-scholarly readers today, however, find them boring; and indeed even scholars may prefer the *Lives of the Poets* or the *Preface to Shakespeare*, where Johnson is giving the quirky personal judgments of a man very much at home with the taste of his own time. But, as everybody knows, the Johnson beloved by "the common reader" is Boswell's conversationalist, a man endowed with almost superhuman vitality, whose most pessimistic remarks are delivered with a vigor that makes a life so intensely lived seem the most precious gift obtainable. It is conceivable that posterity will turn away from Beckett's creative work in the mistaken belief that it is a succession of period pieces indistinguishable in style from the maunderings of his imitators, its pessimism as dated in its own way as the *fin-de-siècle* world-weariness of Huysmans' heroes or the contributors to *The Yellow Book*. Just as Johnson is now best remembered through a posthumous biography of him, so the other Samuel may yet survive in, for example, a posthumous collection of his impatient, incisive, angular, near-illegible letters, whence the telegraphic style of his later prose so clearly derives.

Of one thing at least we can be sure: Beckett will be remembered for different reasons at home and abroad. In France and Germany, Oscar Wilde is best known as the author of *Salomé* or *De Profundis*, whereas in Ireland or England he is most valued for his fairy tales or *The Importance of Being Earnest*. Similarly, Edgar Allan Poe is admired in France for "The Raven" and "The Philosophy of Composition" more than for "To Helen" and the invention of the detective-story. I firmly believe that Beckett's world reputation will in the long run prove greater than Wilde's or Poe's, but the history of its growth in the next century or so may not be exempt from either paradox or dialectic.

2

IRELAND / THE WORLD

"L'artiste qui joue son être est de nulle part," wrote Beckett in "Hommage à Jack B. Yeats."* This might be translated as "The artist who stakes his whole being comes from nowhere." The statement is as true of Beckett himself as it is of Jack Yeats — and as false. Although born in London (29 August 1871), Yeats effectively "came from" Sligo, where he lived with his Pollexfen grandparents from 1879 to 1887, returning to it in memory every day of his life thereafter. Where Beckett comes from — the house where he was born in 1906, which remained his home until his father's death in 1933 — was described recently by a Dublin firm of estate agents in phrases that exude a sober pride, not to say complacency:

> "COOLDRINAGH," BRIGHTON ROAD, FOXROCK, CO. DUBLIN.
> This is a charming Tudor style family residence well set back from the road on the corner of Kerrymount Avenue and standing amid totally secluded mature gardens

* See below, p. 112.

laid out in lawns, tennis court and croquet lawn. This property was designed by Frederick Hicks, architect, and was completed to an extremely high standard of finish. The main rooms face south and west and have spacious proportions and the entire property is in excellent condition. Churches and schools are conveniently situated and there are excellent shops situated in Foxrock Village which is five minutes walk from the property. "Cooldrinagh" is approached by a sweeping gravelled driveway.[1]

Although the house has been added to and modernized somewhat, the original electric-bell indicator, still to be seen in the kitchen in 1975, showed the points to which servants could expect to be summoned during Beckett's early years:

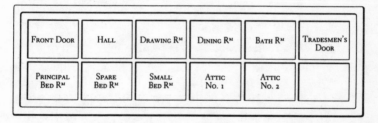

Front Door	Hall	Drawing Rᴹ	Dining Rᴹ	Bath Rᴹ	Tradesmen's Door
Principal Bed Rᴹ	Spare Bed Rᴹ	Small Bed Rᴹ	Attic No. 1	Attic No. 2	

The house (but not its bells) should be compared with that of Mr. Knott in *Watt*. Foxrock Railway Station, now disused, which once served the adjoining Leopardstown Racecourse as well as the village of Foxrock, can easily be recognized as the setting for the concluding pages of *Watt* and much of the action of *All That Fall*.

Samuel Beckett, then, is an Irishman, but to call him an Irish writer involves some semantic sleight of hand. I said of him in an earlier book:

We have the peculiar case here of an Anglo-Irishman
who, like Swift, seems to fit comfortably into the Gaelic
tradition yet has almost no conscious awareness of what
that tradition is.[2]

There were, I suggested, Gaelic elements in the oral culture of English-speaking Ireland that Beckett and Swift had
picked up unconsciously. Perhaps I was to some extent
guilty of special pleading, for an Irish comic tradition that
found no room for Beckett and Swift would hardly have
been worth writing about. Since *The Irish Comic Tradition*
was first published in 1962, however, two important pieces
of evidence about Beckett's attitude to the Irish Literary
Revival have become generally available. As might be expected, they point in opposite directions. On the one hand,
the 1934 article "Recent Irish Poetry" mentioned in the
previous chapter was rescued from pseudonymity in summer 1971 by a Dublin periodical coyly named *The Lace
Curtain*. It revealed that Beckett knew enough about the
Gaelic tradition to mention Oisín, Cuchulain, Maeve, *Tír
na nOg*, the *Táin Bó Cuailnge*, and "the Crone of Beare."
Prompted by a reference in Thomas MacGreevy's poetry,
he even quoted the opening words of Egan O'Rahilly's
most famous poem, "Gile na Gile" ("Brightness of Brightness"), in Irish. He was also aware of Arland Ussher's *The
Midnight Court*, translated from the Irish of Brian Merri-
man. All of this, however, as we have seen, he referred to
only in order to reject it. On the other hand, in *Samuel
Beckett: An Exhibition* (1971), James Knowlson quotes a
letter from Beckett to Cyril Cusack that has some positive
things to say about the drama of the Revival:

I wouldn't suggest that G. B. S. is not a great playwright, whatever that is when it's at home.

What I would do is give the whole unupsettable apple-
cart for a sup of the Hawk's Well, or the Saints', or a
whiff of Juno, to go no further.[3]

This letter was printed in the program for the Shaw Cen-
tenary production of *Androcles and the Lion* at the Gaiety
Theatre, Dublin, in June 1956. It singles out for praise
Yeats's first Noh-style play about Cuchulain, *At the Hawk's
Well*; Synge's play about a blind beggar couple, *The Well
of the Saints*; and O'Casey's Dublin tragicomedy *Juno and
the Paycock*. Beckett preferred the last-mentioned work to
two other O'Casey plays that he had seen at the Abbey
Theatre in his student days: *The Shadow of a Gunman*
and *The Plough and the Stars*.

> Other plays that Beckett remembers having seen at
> this period were Lennox Robinson's *Never the Time
> and the Place* and *The White Blackbird*, and W. B.
> Yeats' two versions of Sophocles (Letter to J. Knowlson,
> 17 December 1970). He is also sure that he saw then
> most of Synge's plays, other Yeats plays and Ibsen's *An
> Enemy of the People*. . . . He also saw Bernard Shaw's
> *Fanny's First Play* at the Abbey.[4]

When one looks for plays analogous to Beckett's in the
Abbey Theatre canon, the names of Synge, O'Casey and
Yeats do in fact come naturally to the mind. The terrified
and terrifying loneliness of Martin and Mary Doul at the
beginning of Act III of *The Well of the Saints*, after they
have become blind again and before they rediscover each
other, recalls similar moments in Beckett. As for O'Casey,

apart from the dialogue in *All That Fall* and *The Old Tune*, it is the "knockabout" element in *Waiting for Godot* and both *Acts Without Words* that most vividly reminds us of him. Beckett himself, in a review of O'Casey's *Windfalls*, which includes two one-act plays, wrote:

> Mr. O'Casey is a master of knockabout in this very serious and honourable sense — that he discerns the principle of disintegration in even the most complacent solidities, and activates it to their explosion. This is the energy of his theatre, the triumph of the principle of knockabout in situation, in all its elements and on all its planes, from the furniture to the higher centres.[5]

Here the Beckett of 1934 seems to be describing the principle of plays that he would not begin to write for another decade.

The Irish plays of the 1920's and 1930's that most resemble Beckett's, however, are by W. B. Yeats: *The Cat and the Moon*, with its blind beggar and lame beggar; *Purgatory*, whose two characters, father and son, hate each other as much as Hamm and Clov do in *Endgame*; and *The Death of Cuchulain*, for the sake of the old man who acts as prologue and has written "certain guiding principles" of dramatic production "on a bit of newspaper."

> I wanted an audience of fifty or a hundred, and if there are more, I beg them not to shuffle their feet or talk when the actors are speaking.[6]

Whether Beckett knew these specific Yeats plays or not, he was certainly aware, according to Francis Warner, of the equally astonishing plays being written at the same time by the poet's brother Jack. Beckett had been a friend of the painter-writer since 1930, and Warner says they used to discuss their writing on long walks together whenever Beckett was in Dublin.[7] Although totally ignorant of this friendship when I first read *En attendant Godot* in 1953, I immediately recalled my impressions of the première of Jack B. Yeats's *La La Noo* at the Abbey on a Sunday night (3 May 1942). The best analysis of the quality shared by these two plays is Robin Skelton's:

> Jack Yeats discovered in *La La Noo*, as Beckett and others discovered later, that the presentation of any event as if it were theatre creates theatre; the frame of the stage is almost all that is needed to give symbolic power to the inconsequent, the casual, the insignificant.[8]

Perhaps this should be emended to read "the *seemingly* inconsequent, the *seemingly* casual," etc. Chapter 4 below suggests how far from casual the structure of the plays can be. Nevertheless, while rejecting certain parts of the Irish literary tradition in his 1934 manifesto, Beckett had implicitly acknowledged his debt to other parts by his 1956 statement.

In the present chapter, it is another aspect of Beckett's Irishness that I want to emphasize: when we remember that he is a special kind of Irishman — Protestant, suburban, middle-class, but brought up and for the most part educated in what is now the Republic — the special kind of universality he seems to communicate to the world at large is more readily understood. To employ two modern clichés, alienation and the search for identity are both serious problems for an Irishman of that heritage. As I wrote in a *New Republic* article in September 1955,

The typical Anglo-Irish boy . . . learns that he is not
quite Irish almost before he can talk; later he learns
that he is far from being English either. The pressure
on him to become either wholly English or wholly
Irish can erase segments of his individuality for good
and all. "Who am I?" is the quetsion that every Anglo-
Irishman must answer, even if it takes him a lifetime, as
it did Yeats.[9]

By editorial request, I used almost identical terms in a *New
Statesman* review of *Molloy* (3 December 1955). Martin
Esslin, in *The Theatre of the Absurd*, disagreed:

It has been suggested that Beckett's preoccupation with
the problems of being and the identity of the self might
have sprung from the Anglo-Irishman's inevitable and
perpetual concern with finding his own answer to the
question 'Who am I?' but while there well may be a
grain of truth in this, it is surely far from providing a
complete explanation for the deep existential anguish
that is the keynote of Beckett's work and that clearly
originates in levels of his personality far deeper than its
social surface.[10]

But indeed I wasn't talking about "social surface": I can't
profess to know for certain what goes on at the deeper levels of my own personality, let alone Beckett's, but something very deep-seated must have prevented me from taking
American citizenship during my thirty-odd years in the
United States. Only half in jest, I keep saying that my
Irish passport is the best proof of my Irishness and, because somebody of my background has such difficulty getting accepted as Irish, I can't afford to give it up. The older
I grow, the more vital it becomes to my psychic health that
I should identify with Ireland — not so much the political

nation as the cultural entity. Perhaps, if I had stayed in
Ireland, I would not have needed to impatriate myself: I
might not have learned Old Irish in my thirties or written
The Irish Comic Tradition. Although — or because — my
Huguenot ancestors came to Ireland over two hundred
years ago, I might have spent my life teaching French language and literature in Irish schools and universities.

Expatriation — whether physical or spiritual — is easy
for people of Beckett's and my background, the so-called
Anglo-Irish, whom I prefer to call Southern Irish Protestants. Historically viewed, we are an intelligentsia as Toyn-
bee defined it in *A Study of History*: a minority group that
draws its ideas and general culture from outside its native
country. Furthermore, our ancestors came to Ireland as
colonists, so that we find it hard to shake off the wariness
and mistrust of the natives proper to a foreign garrison.
That mistrust has the effect sometimes of making conserva-
tives among us take up liberal positions — against censorship and for birth control — in order to stress their difference from Catholics. Because we are colonials, the idea of
a return to the mother country, Great Britain, must always
hold an attraction for some of us, including the kind of
writer who wants a big readership and the power to influence public opinion over a wide area. However, since we
live so close to her, we have fewer illusions about the
mother country than do New Englanders, Canadians, New
Zealanders or Australians.

I have said enough to make it clear that Beckett's Irish
background offered him at least three choices: expatriation,
impatriation, and return to the mother country. A fourth
choice was simply to stay put, as his father and mother and

many of his Protestant contemporaries did, without much
soul-searching about their Irishness. Beckett grew up —
happily, as he insists — in Foxrock, then one of the more
distant and exclusive Dublin suburbs.[11] His neighbors were
mainly well-to-do professional people, many of them Protestant, living in comfortable houses set in their own
grounds. A few were retired British Army officers. Golf was
part of their way of life at a time when Irish golf clubs were
less democratic than they are now. The males and some of
the females of the typical Protestant family took the train
every weekday to office, school or university in Dublin. In
all these places they were likely to be associating almost exclusively with fellow Protestants — as Beckett did at Earls-
fort House School and later at Trinity College. Irish Catholics, rich or poor, played walk-on parts in their lives. The
females who stayed at home spent their leisure time with
other Protestant ladies, though their maids and gardeners
were usually Catholic. If one preferred to think of oneself
as English, there was really no reason not to. The Irish language was not a compulsory subject at Protestant private
schools — Beckett was too old to have been exposed to it
anyway — so that even this rather factitious element of
Irishness was missing.

Staying put, however, is never really a valid option for
anyone self-conscious enough to become an artist. Before
the establishment of the Irish Free State, now the Republic, in 1922, it was certainly possible to return to the mother
country or become an expatriate without anguish. Oscar
Wilde and Bernard Shaw seem to have gone off to England more or less on the spur of the moment. On the other
hand, it cost Synge in particular a great deal of time and

energy to impatriate himself. Interestingly, he first tried expatriation, hoping to earn a living by writing critical articles
on European literature for periodicals in English-speaking
countries. Eventually, as we know, he moved in the opposite direction, impatriating himself at the core of Gaelic
folk culture in the Aran Islands. The resulting creative ex-
plosion suggests that for some years previously he had been
undergoing an identity crisis. W. B. Yeats, on the other
hand, seems to have consciously chosen Irishness without a
struggle.

John Hewitt, the Ulster poet, whose *Collected Poems*
appeared in 1968, has given a very explicit account of his
impatriation. He begins by making the same point about
the Northern Ireland Protestant that I have been making
about his counterpart from the Republic:

> In my experience, people of Planter stock often suffer
> from some crisis of identity, of not knowing where they
> belong. Among us you will find some who call them-
> selves British, some Irish, some Ulstermen, usually with
> a degree of hesitation or mental fumbling.[12]

Given this triple choice, he rejected Irishness because he
was neither Gaelic in speech nor Catholic in religion; Brit-
ishness was no more satisfactory, so he made up his mind
that he was an Ulsterman. For many of the Protestants in
Northern Ireland, who outnumber the Catholics there
two to one, this might have meant no more than staying
put; Hewitt, however, adopted a more positive attitude:

> I set about deepening my knowledge of Ulster's physi-
> cal components, its history, its arts, its literature, its
> folklore. . . .[13]

Ulster is to him a Region — "smaller than the nation, larger than the family" — and he hoped that "in this concept might be found a meeting-place for the two separated communities" of Northern Ireland.[14] This seems a vain hope, but Hewitt's best poems, including long ones like "The Colony" and "Conacre," are based on the exploration of what it is to be an Ulsterman.

Did Beckett undergo a similar crisis of identity? It seems certain that he did, and that it was painful and prolonged, lasting from about 1930, when he returned from his two years' teaching in Paris, until at least 1937. In a deeper sense, as Esslin suggested, Beckett's identity crisis has been lifelong, but during the years 1930-37 he oscillated between Dublin on the one hand and London, Paris, Germany on the other before finally settling in Paris.* Lawrence E. Harvey describes Beckett's predicament at this period as follows:

> Caught between the two impossibilities of domestication and exile and unfailing in filial devotion, he found return and departure almost equally painful — and equally desirable — alternatives.[15]

Harvey's "domestication" is what I have termed "staying put," and in his view the only valid alternative was expatriation. When Beckett gave up his post as lecturer in French at Trinity, after only four terms (quarters), at the end of 1931, he was probably also rejecting the Foxrock world — of which Trinity was in many ways a continuation — at least at the unconscious level. But, after a vain attempt to

---

* Since Beckett is of Huguenot descent on his father's side, one might describe this — not very seriously — as a return to *la patrie* though not to the mother country.

support himself in Paris and London, he went back to
Foxrock before the end of 1932. In June 1933 his father
died, quite unexpectedly, after a brief illness. Beckett's
elder brother then allowed him £200 a year for the good-
will of his interest in the family firm. Beckett, now independent though poor, spent three unhappy years in London
and some six months in Germany before returning to Paris
in autumn 1937.[16] He was settling there for good, though he
probably did not know this at the time. The way was opening to a self-discovery in expatriation at least as startling as
Synge's in impatriation. Synge first visited the Aran Islands in May 1898; by the end of 1902, he had written two
one-act plays that are part of world theater; by 1907 he had
completed his two masterpieces, *The Well of the Saints*
and *The Playboy of the Western World*. Having begun to
write in French in 1945, Beckett by the end of 1950 had
completed *Premier amour*, the three *Nouvelles*, *Mercier et
Camier*, *Molloy*, *Malone meurt*, *L'Innommable*, *En attendant Godot*, and the *Textes pour rien*: the great majority of
the work on which his reputation as a French writer depends.

Why was it that Beckett never seriously considered the
possibility of avoiding alienation by impatriating himself?
The first reason that occurs to me is a paradoxical one: unlike myself, he had never lived in or perhaps even visited
any part of Ireland where he was unpleasantly conscious of
minority or alien status. Portora Royal School, Enniskillen,
County Fermanagh, which he attended for three and a half
years as a boarder, was then exclusively Protestant. Even
after the establishment of the Irish Free State, he could
hardly have felt like an alien in this Northern Ireland

school, since at least half of the boarders during E. G.
Seale's headmastership were from below the Border. The
day-boys, it is true, guaranteed a Northern majority, but
they counted for little in the life of the boarders. (As I
entered Portora as a boarder in 1928, five years after Beckett
went up to Trinity, I am making these generalizations on
the basis of my own experience.) I assume that Beckett
never underwent the minor ordeal that I endured daily
when at home in Clara, Offaly, of walking past a row of
half-doors over which stared ironic Irish eyes — not those
of romanticizable peasants but of sharp-tongued women,
girls and boys, the wives and children of factory-workers,
who knew more about me and my family than I would ever
know about them. I never could decide whether I hated
them or longed to be accepted by them: as I went to a one-
teacher Protestant school while they went to big schools
taught by nuns and monks, there really was no common
ground for us to meet on.

Another reason why Beckett may never have considered
impatriating or Gaelicizing himself is supplied by the late-
ness and foreignness of his intellectual awakening. At Portora, although he was already showing talent in English and
French composition, he made his mark chiefly as an ath-
lete: a good swimmer, a fair boxer, a member of the rugby
football first fifteen, and above all a brilliant cricketer,
playing for the first eleven from the age of fourteen. He
showed no signs of rebellion against his class or his culture
and if he had intellectual or artistic ambitions, he kept
them to himself. When he entered Trinity College, Dublin, in October 1923, he was seventeen and a half, about a

year younger than average. Either because his family was comfortably off or because his masters did not think he had enough ability, he was not kept back a year and trained like a racehorse for the Junior Exhibition (entrance scholarship) examinations. He took the examinations, but did not win an exhibition. Two Portorans, O. W. McCutcheon and G. P. Stewart, won Junior Exhibitions in 1923, but two years later, when Beckett makes his first appearance in the Trinity "red calendar" as a prizewinner, he is ranked sixth among the Senior Exhibitioners, Stewart being in fourth place and McCutcheon fifth. The same year, 1925, Beckett played cricket for the Trinity first eleven, winning his "pink," an athletic award that is the equivalent of an Oxford or Cambridge "blue," the next year. In the 1926 Scholarship examinations, Beckett took fourth place in Modern Languages to McCutcheon (first) and two women students, while Stewart stood first in Mental and Moral Science (Philosophy). It was not until the Moderatorship (Honors B.A.) examinations in 1927 that Beckett came into his own: first of First Class in Modern Literature, with McCutcheon in fourth place and Stewart second of First Class in Mental and Moral Science.[17]

These results need interpretation: for example, the Senior Exhibition proves versatility only, the ability to win high marks in three or four subjects and pass in two or three more. Some brilliant but one-sided undergraduates had the greatest difficulty in merely passing "Little-go" — now happily abolished — because they were strong in languages and weak in the sciences and mathematics or vice versa. As for the compulsory paper and *viva voce* (oral) examination in scholastic logic, everybody scrambled through with the help of the time-honored mnemonic that Beckett imperfectly recalls in Chapter 2 of *Murphy*:

> as Murphy had shown her many times in Barbara, Baccardi [Bocardo] and Baroko, though never in Bramantip.

The Scholarship result may simply mean that McCutcheon had taken both French and German at Portora, whereas Beckett had studied only French, beginning Italian after he entered Trinity.

It seems hardly possible, however, that Beckett would have made the effort necessary to place himself at the head of his year if he had not been set afire intellectually by French and Italian literature, and particularly by Dante and Racine. I remember being surprised by the intensity of Beckett's admiration for our former French professor, T. B. Rudmose-Brown, when I first heard him express it, but "Ruddy" was of course responsible for introducing him to Racine and may well have been the first to suggest that scholarship offered pleasure as well as pain. As for Dante — perhaps the greatest single literary influence on his own so different work — Beckett does not now remember whether Dr. Walter Starkie or Sir Robert Tate guided his first steps in that labyrinth. He does remember that he "worked a lot" on the *Divine Comedy* with Signorina Bianca Esposito, daughter of the pianist, presumably the original of Signorina Adriana Ottolenghi in "Dante and the Lobster." In the letter of 15 October 1976 conveying this information, he also assured me that he had never contributed to the school magazine while at Portora, nor had he ever submitted a contribution to *T.C.D.: A College Miscellany*

during his undergraduate years at Trinity. (His few post-
graduate contributions, beginning in November 1929, are
well documented.) These facts suggest that Beckett may
be that rare, almost unique, creature — a literary artist
whose first ambitions were scholarly rather than creative.

Even so, during his first two years in college Beckett was
probably more interested in cricket and golf than in his
studies, though he did well enough in the latter; his intellectual life, properly speaking, may not yet have begun.
Winning a Foundation Scholarship entitled him to rooms
in the College, whereas previously he had lived at home.
His moving into these in the autumn of 1926 and the simultaneous arrival of Alfred Péron from the Ecole Normale
Supérieure as exchange lecturer in French marked an epoch
in Beckett's life, both socially and intellectually. When
W. S. Maguinness returned to Trinity in October 1927
after a year's absence — he had won the Classical Student-
ship, a traveling scholarship, in 1926 — he noticed the
change at once. Beckett had begun not only to hold opin-
ions but to express them and was ready to argue about
whatever intellectuals argued about in 1927. He had also
learned to take a drink, or several. Maguinness attributed all
these changes to the friendship with Péron, though Beckett could easily have learnt conviviality from his athletic
friends.[18]

Beckett reached intellectual self-awareness, it seems, at
a somewhat late age compared with James Joyce or fellow
Protestants like Yeats and Synge: he did so, furthermore,
under Continental influences, both literary and personal.
(Thomas Brown Rudmose-Brown was a Scotsman, as it
happens, but the cultural revival in which he was most in-

terested was that of the *langue d'oc;* he taught some Provençal language and literature at Trinity in his last years.) These influences were reinforced when, after two terms of teaching at Portora's rival school, Campbell College, in Belfast, Beckett went to Paris in October 1928 for two years as exchange lecturer at the Ecole Normale Supérieure. Thomas MacGreevy, his predecessor in that post, almost immediately introduced him to Joyce, and the next year Beckett contributed his Opus One, "Dante . . . Bruno . Vico . . Joyce," to the famous symposium, *Our Examination Round His Factification for Incamination of Work in Progress.* The same year he published a short story, "Assumption," in *Transition,* the Paris avant-garde magazine that was by now publishing Joyce's *Work in Progress* in fairly regular installments. In 1930 came his prize-winning poem *Whoroscope,* a pastiche of Eliot and Pound, larded with quotations and allusions that had to be explained in notes. Usually a poet begins by imitating the classics of his language: Beckett, on the contrary, caught up with the international avant-garde on his first flight. No wonder he had a great deal to unlearn later. He was to tell Gabriel d'Aubarède in a 1961 interview: "I'm no intellectual. All I am is feeling. *Molloy* and the others came to me the day I became aware of my own folly. Only then did I begin to write the things I feel."[19]

His greatest folly consisted in attempting to imitate James Joyce: not the earlier work, either, but *Work in Progress,* the drafts of *Finnegans Wake.* Two squibs in *T.C.D.*, "Che Sciagura" and "The Possessed," can be condoned as parodies, but "Sedendo et Quiescendo," published in *Transition* for March 1932, is evidently intended

to be taken seriously. It presents, in a stream-of-conscious-
ness style that stands halfway between *Ulysses* and *Finnegans Wake*, a journey to Germany undertaken by Belacqua
and his reunion there with Smeraldina; both characters
later appear in *More Pricks Than Kicks*. One wonders
whether Joyce encouraged Beckett to make such experiments with form, forgetting the slow, painful way in which
he himself had progressed from *Chamber Music* and the
early stories in *Dubliners*, via the long gestation of *A Portrait of the Artist as a Young Man*, to the formal virtuosity
of the later episodes in *Ulysses*. Joyce may never have even
suspected that, while his own hoard of Irish knowledge and
feeling was virtually inexhaustible, Beckett had brought
from his carefully insulated suburban community little
that was usable and durable. Foxrock deliberately avoided
much of Irish popular culture while providing regrettably
little English culture, high or low, to put in its place. "A
Wet Night" in *More Pricks Than Kicks* seems to boast
how cosmopolitan and cultivated is the Dublin Beckett
knows, yet the conversation never for a moment becomes
interesting, whereas that of the half-educated native Dubliners in Joyce's "Grace" or "Ivy Day in the Committee
Room" holds the reader spellbound. Much of Beckett's
later work is the result of a continuous process of stripping,
peeling and paring away: he has learned that for him at
least the secret of universality lies not in being able to
write in several languages at once or to parade before the
reader characters belonging to half a dozen different nation-
alities — as in "A Wet Night" — but in presenting, to use
Lear's words, "the thing itself; unaccommodated man . . .
no more but such a poor, bare, forked animal as thou art."

It could be argued that the banning of *More Pricks Than Kicks* in the Irish Free State was crucial in alienating Beckett from Ireland. Lawrence Harvey quotes an unpublished essay dating from 1936, "Censorship in the Saorstat [Free State]," in which Beckett denounces both censorship and the prohibition of birth control, saying: "Sterilisation of the mind and apotheosis of the litter suit well together."[20] He was particularly indignant at the banning of books as "in general tendency indecent or obscene" by censorship board members who read only marked passages in the works submitted to them, taking the part for the whole. At one point in *Murphy* he writes: "This phrase is chosen with care, lest the filthy censors should lack an occasion to commit their filthy synecdoche." Even before the order prohibiting his book had been made by the Irish Free State Minister for Justice, however, Beckett had gone on record in "Recent Irish Poetry" as rejecting "the *Gossoons Wunderhorn* [*Des Knaben Wunderhorn*] of that Irish Romantic Arnim-Brentano combination, Sir Samuel Ferguson and Standish O'Grady. . . ." The article's purpose was not in fact entirely negative: Beckett was consciously making propaganda for a group of Irish modernist poets, some of them contributors to *Transition*, that included himself, though he does not say so. The poets of whom he approves include Blanaid Salkeld, Percy (Arland) Ussher, Lyle Donaghy, Geoffrey Taylor and Thomas MacGreevy, whom he calls "an existentialist in verse, the Titchener of the modern lyric." Edward Bradford Titchener (1867-1927) was an important figure in the early history of experimental psychology; we cannot therefore be certain that Beckett had been reading Heidegger. In any case, he was more concerned with literary influences than with philosophical or psychological ones. At the end of his review / manifesto, he singled out Denis Devlin and Brian Coffey as

> without question the most interesting of the youngest generation of Irish poets. . . . they have submitted themselves to the influences of those poets least concerned with evading the bankrupt relationship referred to at the opening of this essay — Corbière, Rimbaud, Laforgue, the *surréalistes* and Mr. Eliot, perhaps also to those of Mr. Pound — with results that constitute already the nucleus of a living poetic in Ireland. . . .[21]

Ironically, none of these recommended poets except Denis Devlin — and he only to a small degree — succeeded in gaining the ear of that international audience to which, in the final analysis, they were addressing themselves. Beckett succeeded where they had failed, but not because of his lyric poetry. On the whole, W. B. Yeats was right and Beckett wrong: by cutting themselves off from a native tradition, these Irish poets of the 1930's condemned themselves to pastiche. Austin Clarke, a *bête noire* to Beckett, by persisting in his Irishness eventually became, like Yeats before him, a model for poets fifty years his juniors.

Beckett's natural gifts as a writer would probably in the end have triumphed over any convention in which he chose to write. *Murphy,* for all its self-conscious cleverness, its pedantry, its cosmopolitan eclecticism, contains passages, especially in Chapter 6 (on Murphy's mind) and Chapter 13 (the last), that deal existentially with the human condition. But the true source of strength in Beckett's later works is his total acceptance of expatriation. Alienated, however unconsciously at first, from the majority of his fellow citizens of the Free State, he made alienation into a way of life: first in London during the unhappy years that produced *Murphy*, then in Paris. His wartime experience pushed him still farther along the path of alienation. He became estranged from his native tongue to the point where, like Nabokov, he could not merely write in a foreign language but be recognized as an inimitable — though often imitated — stylist in it. Circumstances had combined to make him an alienated artist: his own genius was to make him a fit laureate for an age of alienation. By the end of the war he must have realized that a man of his caliber could not be content — as I, a critic, can be — with a mere identification of himself as an Irishman or a Frenchman. Identity lay far deeper than identification: I am a man, yes, but what do I mean by "I" or "man"? *The Unnamable*, a novel about the impossibility and yet the necessity of saying "I," represents the final stage possible in that search for identity. Beyond lies annihilation, the loss of all being: Beckett looked at it in *Endgame* but could not accept it.

As we saw in the previous chapter, after finishing the French original of *Endgame*, Beckett wrote his first major original work in English since *Watt: All That Fall*, "a text written to come out of the dark."[22] Both *Watt* and *All That Fall* are set in and around Foxrock, but, as several critics have shown, many of the French works too have Irish settings, though not such precise ones. Marilyn Gaddis Rose, in a perceptive article entitled "The Irish Memories of Beckett's Voice," has pointed out Irish topographical allusions in works that might seem totally free of time and place: *Textes pour rien*, for example, and *Comment c'est*.[23] I will have more to say about this aspect of the French works in the next chapter, but one or two details that would catch the eye of a Dubliner and yet sound quite unspecific to a Londoner or a Parisian ought to be set down here as examples of the dialectic between the local and the universal. For instance, in *Texts for Nothing* VII we find the following passages:

> And what if all this time I had not stirred hand or foot from the third class waiting-room of the South-Eastern Railway Terminus, I never dared wait first on a third class ticket, and were still there waiting to leave, for the south-east, the south rather, east lay the sea. . . .

> But tut there I am far again from that terminus and its pretty neo-Doric colonnade. . . .

This is not just any rail terminus, of course, but Harcourt Street Station, Dublin, where the suburban trains arrived from and departed to Foxrock. Though the building is no longer a railway station, its colonnade still remains to be admired.

Many readers of *Mercier et Camier* and its English translation have failed to grasp either that it is set in Ireland or that its "heroes" are Irish: the one follows from the other, for in the second paragraph of the first chapter we are told:

> Mercier and Camier did not remove from home, they had that great good fortune. They did not have to face, with greater or less success, outlandish ways, tongues, laws, skies, foods. . . . The weather, though often inclement (but they knew no better), never exceeded the limits of the temperate. . . .

We first see them together in a square named after "a Field Marshal of France peacefully named Saint-Ruth." Admit-

tedly, there is no square in Dublin or anywhere else in Ireland named after Maréchal St.-Ruth, but every Irish schoolboy knows that he died in Ireland at the Battle of Aughrim.
All sorts of small details, such as the coins used, are Irish
rather than French, especially in the original: for example,
Mercier and Camier bring *une bouteille de J.J.* (John Jame-
son's Irish whiskey) to their hotel room. Some of the details, however, are blurred or omitted in Beckett's translation. At the beginning of Chapter VII, he omits the second
sentence of the corresponding chapter (No. X) in the
French: "C'est l'ancien chemin des armées." Most Dubliners know or have heard of the Old Military Road, built to
hunt Irish rebels in County Wicklow. Many also know the
plain cross, planted in the bog not far from that road, which
Camier sees. The narrator tells us that it marks "the grave
of a nationalist. . . . His name was Masse, perhaps Mas-
sey." The French says only, "Il s'appelait Masse." The murdered man's real surname was Lemass, and he was of Huguenot descent. So, of course, is Beckett; so, of course, are
those sterling Irishmen Mercier and Camier: it is probably
no coincidence that a Mercier (myself) and a Camier had
followed Beckett from Portora to Trinity long before the
year 1946, in which he wrote *Mercier et Camier.*

It should be stressed that when Beckett does write directly in English, he rarely makes use of Irish dialect. In
Watt and *All That Fall,* only the working-class characters
— the railway-station staff and the man driving the cart
loaded with manure — speak in dialect. I can't detect anything distinctively Irish in the speech of his middle-class
characters except for Mr. Gorman and Mr. Cream in *The
Old Tune:* they use a number of Dublin expressions that

can also be found in the works of O'Casey and Joyce — and perhaps a few that can't. Ironically, this most Irish of his plays is adapted from *La Manivelle*, a play in highly colloquial French by Robert Pinget.[24] About Beckett's own spoken English, as opposed to that of his characters, there can be no shadow of doubt: although he uses only an occasional dialect expression, and then for deliberate effect, his voice has a distinctly Dublin quality of the kind often described as "a Trinity accent," though neither Joyce nor Shaw, who both also spoke in this way, went to Trinity. Most Trinity men, in fact, don't have this accent: it belongs to middle-class Dubliners who live on the South Side of the River Liffey; unless you or your parents grew up in the Georgian squares or the red-brick suburbs, you are very unlikely to pick it up. W. B. Yeats, for example, never had it: although born in the South Dublin suburb of Sandymount, he spoke with the accent of Sligo.

Three great Dublin writers besides Beckett have made their homes in Paris for shorter or longer periods, been much influenced by French literature, and received much admiration from the French: Oscar Wilde, John Synge, James Joyce. Beckett has something in common with each of them, but the differences in his work and personality are crucial.

Wilde came from the Dublin professional class, went to Portora and Trinity, and wrote a play in French for the Paris stage. He seems a typical expatriate dilettante, trying to imitate the French avant-garde of his day, but succeeding only superficially. *The Picture of Dorian Gray* is a vulgarization of Huysmans' *A rebours*; Wilde's attempts at *symboliste* poetry are Swinburne and water; *Salomé* may be decadent, but it is still melodrama. None of this is any better than Beckett's early poems or *More Pricks Than Kicks*, and there is nothing to suggest that if Wilde had lived longer he would have gone deeper. His best work was done for the London stage in the tradition of Congreve and Sheridan — a colonist returning to the mother country. It is Wilde the man rather than Wilde the artist who has achieved universality.

Synge, like Beckett, came from a more puritanical, less sophisticated Protestant home than Wilde. Unlike Beckett, he was lonely at Trinity. After some years of expatriation, Synge, as we have seen, impatriated himself. He did not, as Beckett implied in "Recent Irish Poetry," fly from self-awareness to an Aran idyll: on the contrary, Aran helped him to confront both himself and the human condition. Act II of *The Well of the Saints*, properly understood, is the grimmest confrontation of all: Martin Doul, having been cured of blindness, literally *sees* that life is nasty, brutish, short. Synge found universality not in Mallarmé or Huysmans or even Pierre Loti but in Irish myth and folklore and folk life.

Joyce managed to have it both ways: he was an expatriate avant-garde artist who imagined that he was casting aside his family, his nationality and his religion; but, just as he brought one of his brothers and two of his sisters to Europe to live with him, so he kept his country and his church in his baggage too. The universality of *Ulysses* at least, and probably that of the other works too, depends on parochialism. A glance at the names and addresses in the visitors' book at the martello tower in Sandycove ought to convince anyone who doubts this. People come from all over the world to visit a military relic at a suburban bathing place because a young Dublin man once spent a few days there and stamped his image forever upon the opening pages of his greatest work.

It seems unlikely that there will ever be a holy place of pilgrimage like Yeats's tower or Joyce's tower in any posthumous Beckett cult. The "necessary house . . . on the right as one goes down into the pit" has disappeared with the rest of the old Abbey Theatre, while the "breakdown of the object" in Beckett's own work almost guarantees that no other place less suited to subjective reverie is likely to capture the imagination of his readers. "Cooldrinagh," Foxrock, lacks charisma in itself and has had little bestowed on it by his works. Nor are the places where he lived in Paris and London likely to attract the crowd. Dublin, London, Paris, all lie on the circumference; as he made clear in 1934, the center is what counts. While Beckett still lives, his mind is the center; after his death it will be found in his books. He has traveled farther than most men towards the center of his own being; more important still, he has been able to come back and "record his findings."[25] We who read his books and watch his plays have been able to recognize ourselves in this or that part of his findings and thus are or ought to be prepared to take the rest on trust. Beckett's universality, in the last analysis, does not depend on impatriation or expatriation, on Irishness, Frenchness or cosmopolitanism: it depends on the paradox of a unique self that has found its bedrock in our common human predicament.

3

GENTLEMAN / TRAMP

I once remarked to Samuel Beckett that I thought it odd of him to translate the colloquial French "Ce serait un moyen de bander" as "We'd get an erection." It seemed to me, I said, that here and elsewhere in the English version of *En attendant Godot* he made Didi and Gogo sound as if they had earned Ph.D.'s. "How do you know they hadn't?" was his answer. Like most playgoers and readers, I was so accustomed to thinking of Beckett's characters in general as what the English would call "tramps," the Americans "bums," and the Irish "traveling men" perhaps, that I had failed to remember the ambiguity of such terms. No doubt some men are born tramps ("ditch-delivered by a drab"), but others achieve tramp-hood or have it thrust upon them. It was particularly inexcusable for me to miss this point, since I had read *More Pricks Than Kicks* and *Murphy* — the protagonists of which were clearly not tramps — long before Beckett burst onto the world literary scene in the early 1950's. Whether a French intellectual had read *Molloy* and

Malone meurt before seeing *En attendant Godot* or afterwards, the net effect would have been the same: an impression of almost totally deprived characters, without proper lodging, proper clothes, proper food, or even the full use of their minds and bodies.

And yet when one looks at photographs of the first Paris staging of *Godot*, apparently supervised with care by Beckett, one sees that both Vladimir and Estragon are more shabby-genteel than ragged.[1] A stage direction mentions Estragon's "rags" (*haillons*), but the pair are dressed in intact though far from pristine dark clothes. Vladimir actually wears a stiff collar and a tie; although Estragon wears a scarf round his neck and presumably no collar, the fact that both wear intact bowler hats suggests they still have aspirations to gentility. Of course, both the pathos and the humor of the tramp portrayed by Charlie Chaplin depend upon his similar aspirations: his bowler hat, dark jacket and walking-stick strive to be genteel, but the ill-fitting trousers and boots give the show away. His politeness, especially to women, strikes us as excessive; we wonder if perhaps his parents trained him in it because they had "ideas above their station in life": a genuine aristocrat might be far less obsequious. We never discover, though, whether Charlie has come down in the world or is merely trying to rise in it: like all the great clown figures, he has no past and his future is an illusion; he exists in a perpetual present. The same at first seems to be true of Molloy, Malone, Didi, Gogo, but in fact they and almost all the other Beckett characters have pasts. "Hamm as stated, and Clov as stated, together as stated . . ."[2] may be true of those two characters in *Endgame*, but Nagg and Nell in the same play have a common past — perhaps largely illusory, since they claim they were happy then — about which they speak quite often.

Since the popular conception of the archetypal Beckett character arises primarily from the three works *Waiting for Godot, Molloy,* and *Malone Dies,* it will be worthwhile to establish with some care the extent to which their leading characters can be said to have "come down in the world" in a social and economic sense as well as a psychological or even moral one. Very early in *Godot,* as a matter of fact, when Vladimir first speaks of suicide, we learn that "a million years ago, in the nineties," he and Estragon were both respectable. They ought to have ended it all then, "Hand in hand from the top of the Eiffel Tower, among the first. We were presentable in those days. Now it's too late. They wouldn't even let us up." This is one of very few references to their past. Another is also connected with suicide: Estragon asks, "Do you remember the day I threw myself into the Rhône?" Vladimir remembers that they were grape-harvesting at the time, which certainly doesn't suggest affluence. But of course the chief argument in favor of their having had a comfortable upbringing is, as my remark to Beckett suggested, the way they speak. Although they don't know where they are or what day of the week it is, they can talk intelligently in a large vocabulary on a variety of subjects. Within a passage of a few lines, Gogo compares them to caryatids and Didi uses the Latin tag *Memoria praeteritorum bonorum.* Apart from the Bible (and the maps of the Holy Land in Estragon's copy of it), it is hard to put one's finger on anything specific they have read or studied; Estragon does, however, adapt Shelley's "To the Moon":

> Art thou pale for weariness
> Of climbing heaven and gazing on the earth . . .?

There is no equivalent quotation in the French, at this point or elsewhere, but it seems likely that Beckett inserted this passage into the English quite self-consciously, so as to leave no doubt that Didi and Gogo are not merely "nature's gentlemen" but have received some formal education. The extreme politeness that they show from time to time might have resulted from their being trained as waiters, say, but Vladimir at least is capable of being scandalized, not only on moral grounds (by Pozzo's inhuman treatment of Lucky) but on a matter of etiquette when Estragon begs for chicken bones or money.

In *Molloy*, it is natural to contrast Molloy's final state in Part I with Moran's initial state in Part II. But in fact Molloy may have fallen even farther than Moran eventually will. If we look closely, we see that, except in regard to theology perhaps, Molloy has received a wider and deeper education than the completely middle-class Moran. Leaving aside the question whether *toute honte bue* is a reminiscence of François Villon or whether "It is in the tranquillity of decomposition that I remember the long confused emotion which was my life . . ." is an allusion to Wordsworth, we can find a number of unambiguously learned references in Molloy's narrative: "Belacqua, or Sordello, I forget"; "The Times Literary Supplement"; "Geulincx"; "the famous fatal skin," in French *la fameuse peau de chagrin*, of Balzac; "Galileo's vessels." He is almost sure that *nimis sero* is Latin for "too late" and uses the tag *Homo mensura** almost unconsciously. Whether he knows that

* *Homo mensura omnium*: Man, the measure of all things.

twenty-two divided by seven is an approximation of pi or not, he certainly knows that it leads to a recurring decimal: "and the pages fill with the true ciphers at last." Compared with this range of humanistic culture, Moran's reference to "the great Gustave" Flaubert and his use of the German phrase *Sollst entbehren* ("Thou shalt do without") seem insignificant, even when we add to them the knotty theological questions offered later in the novel. Moran may have attended a seminary, but Molloy has received a liberal education, whence perhaps his "passion for truth." We are prepared to accept his own statement that he has at different times studied — or at least taken an interest in — astronomy, geology, anthropology, psychiatry and magic.

Malone does not make free with great names so frequently as Molloy does, but his culture is broad. It includes some knowledge of art history, since he writes of "such a night as Kaspar David Friedrich loved, tempestuous and bright" and seems to allude to Watteau's *L'Embarquement pour Cythère*. He knows enough Latin to quote Lucretius' *Suave mari magno* in an appropriate context, and enough philosophy to quote "*Nihil in intellectu,* etc." Sordello appears again, and Malone further shows his range by making a confident assertion about "mystic texts."

Molloy has not only the education but also the manners of a gentleman, at least sporadically, in spite of implying that he has "always behaved like a pig." He likes to be treated courteously, remarking that a police sergeant "began to interrogate me in a tone which, from the point of view of civility, left increasingly to be desired, in my opinion." Because of his mother's blindness and deafness, he has to treat her rather rudely, but he imagines himself "saying to a passer-by, doffing my hat, I beg your pardon, Sir, this *is* X, is it not?" Perhaps he is not to be taken too seriously on the one occasion when he describes himself as a gentleman: "I give you my word, I cannot piss, my word of honour, as a gentleman." Nevertheless, in almost his last words to us he demonstrates his gentlemanly instincts. He is telling us how his hat had become jammed on his head: "And if I had met any lady friends, if I had had any lady friends, I would have been powerless to salute them correctly."

Both Molloy and Malone share the view that clothes make the man. They, like most Beckett characters, feel that the only appropriate head-covering for a man is a bowler — *un chapeau melon* or, in Anglo-Irish phrase, "a block-hat." Chaplin's tramp felt the same way, but so, apparently, did Beckett's father, at any rate when he went to a race meeting.[3] A notable exception to this rule is Moran, who wears a "straw boater." Almost all these characters are attached to their hats in a quasi-literal sense, the hat being attached by a lace or string to a lapel of the greatcoat; here again, Moran shows his lack of aristocratic tone, holding his boater on by an elastic under his chin. For the attachment of a hard hat to a lapel is a mark of the fox-hunting man, who is otherwise likely to lose his headgear while jumping a hedge or a ditch. Malone says of the hat worn by Macmann and "attached, by a string, for safety, to the topmost button of the coat" that "it would not surprise me to learn that this hat once belonged to a sporting gentleman." Evidently Macmann was not himself that gentleman, since his head is too big for the hat, whereas the "toff's" head was "small from over-breeding." But if Macmann is not well-bred, his creator, Malone, certainly knows what breeding is; his sense of decorum is deeply ingrained. After describing the visit to his room of a man whom he at first takes to be an undertaker's assistant because he wears a black suit, black tie and block-hat, he comes to the moment when the man takes fright and steps away from the bed: "It was then I saw he was wearing brown boots, which gave me such a shock as no words can convey." No words of mine, either, can convey the priceless humor of such a remark. Here is a man at the point of death, who suspects he is being measured for his coffin, yet the only thing capable of shocking him is the wearing of brown boots with a black suit!

Beckett's handling of these sartorial details and my comments on them should be viewed in the serio-comic spirit of Carlyle's *Sartor Resartus*. They do, however, force upon us the conclusion that Beckett's tragicomic figures are down-at-heel gentry rather than *Lumpenproletariat* and that our attitudes towards them should be modified accordingly. The plays and novels cannot therefore be consistently interpreted as versions of pastoral or pleas for the downtrodden: instead they link up with an Anglo-Irish literary tradition at least as old as Maria Edgeworth's *Castle Rackrent*. Not only the bodies but the minds of Molloy, Malone, Vladimir and Estragon are clad in "relics of ould dacency." They were not born into the landed gentry, like the decaying heroes of Edgeworth and Somerville and Ross, but it is reasonable to argue that they came from the professional classes — prone, in Ireland as in England, to ape the manners of the aristocracy while possessing a better education than they.

There is one character in Beckett who is presented un-

equivocally as a landlord: Pozzo in *Waiting for Godot.*
Here again the costuming of the first production reinforces
the hint given us by Pozzo's insistence that Didi and Gogo
are on his land. Pozzo is dressed like the wicked landlord of
Victorian melodrama: a sporty, light-colored bowler; riding
breeches and leggings; a handsome check overcoat, more
cloak than coat. Some of the details are French rather than
English or Irish, but Pozzo would be immediately recognized as a landlord in a play about Victorian Ireland. As for
Lucky, he combines elements of the downtrodden Irish
peasant and the French *laquais.* (Beckett originally wanted
him dressed as a railway porter but accepted Roger Blin's
suggestions.) His tail-coat is ornamented with braid and
his horizontally striped jersey resembles that of a French
sailor, but his knee breeches unfastened at the knee, his
bare legs, and what look like buckled shoes recall the nineteenth-century Irish peasant of *Punch* cartoons. I am surprised that Marxist critics have not paid more attention to
the searing caricature of exploitation by one class or race of
another that is represented in the Pozzo-Lucky relationship.
This is not the place to analyze it in detail, but Pozzo's insistence on the goodness of his own heart and the dog-like
devotion to him of Lucky are as familiar in the mythology
of the Irish landlord class as they were in that of the planta-
tion owner in the Old South.

Any reader who has followed my argument this far, however, will be quick to object that Lucky too, far from being
an illiterate peasant, shows marks of having fallen from a
higher estate. It is possible, of course, that his famous monologue when ordered to "think" is a garbled recollection of
something learned by rote, but the rote learning of an illit-

erate tends to come out word-perfect. Might not Lucky once have been able to think independently, a faculty that he has since lost through ill-treatment, malnutrition and perhaps psychosis? Many Irish peasants were the dispossessed descendants of learned or ruling families, just as some Roman slaves were Greek intellectuals who became the tutors of aristocrats and future emperors.

Let us turn now, briefly, to the characters in Beckett's other major works. First, the protagonists of *More Pricks Than Kicks* and *Murphy*. Belacqua Shuah in the former belongs to the upper middle class by birth at least: in the first and best of this series of tales, he is studying Dante with a private tutor and has an aunt who serves him lobster; need one say more? Murphy is an ex-clerical student — unemployable, no doubt, as Beckett felt he himself was, but living on money supplied by "a Dutch uncle," just as his creator for a long time lived on £200 a year derived from the family business.

The protagonist of *Watt* is described by Ludovic Janvier as "premier en date des clochards mythiques,"[4] but here again one must ask for more precision: *clochard* ("tramp") Watt may be, but his mind is capable of extraordinarily rigorous logic while he is at Mr. Knott's house, and one of the notes not incorporated into the novel credits him with being able to recognize a chord, "C major in its second inversion," simply by looking at a picture of a man playing a piano. Early in the book, Mrs. Nixon says of him, "He is a university man, of course." Mr. Nixon replies, "I should think it highly probable." The title characters of *Mercier et Camier*, however shabby, come from the middle classes and seem to possess an unearned income. The still-unpublished play *Eleuthéria* deals in a fairly conventional way with the rebellion of Victor Krap against the conventionality of his bourgeois parents. If I am correct in believing that the voice in *The Unnamable* belongs to a soul that has never been born, then the protagonist of this work has no *état civil* and can't be discussed within a social frame of reference. Hamm in *Endgame*, like Pozzo, is a master and has a servant, even if Clov is also his son. Hamm claims that the house where all the characters live is his. In the past, he must have owned or been in charge of quite a large area, for he speaks of Clov going on rounds to inspect "my paupers"; these rounds were made "Sometimes on horse."

It is a little ridiculous to speak in such terms of a play like *Endgame*, set in an indefinite future time that could be described as timeless. The radio plays *All That Fall* and *Embers*, on the other hand, have very specific though unidentified locations in space and time. Mr. and Mrs. Rooney of *All That Fall* live in a suburb from which Mr. Rooney commutes daily by train to the city. The railway station, like that in *Watt*, adjoins a racecourse, suggesting the station serving Beckett's native Foxrock and the nearby Leopardstown track. The period is after the invention of the motor car. If we are to take Mr. Rooney's calculations seriously, he earns only about £2 a week yet pays £12 a year for his season ticket alone. Clearly he is losing money by going to the city every day. But in all probability, since he owns a house in a desirable location, he has a private income. Henry in *Embers* is unequivocally well-to-do. He has inherited money from his father and set up house near the sea on the opposite side of the bay to his paternal home. He seems to have no profession or business yet can afford to

visit Switzerland and pay for piano and riding lessons for
his daughter.

As for the protagonist of *Krapp's Last Tape*, he is a man
of independent means, whether he lives in a suburb or not.
He can afford to dedicate his life to producing his *opus
magnum*, of which seventeen copies have been sold. He
wears a "heavy" silver watch and chain, drinks too much,
and can pay a prostitute to visit his house from time to
time. His *"surprising pair of dirty white boots . . . very
narrow and pointed"* suggest the ex-dandy rather than the
former cricketer. With *Happy Days* we are once again in a
timeless future, but Winnie and Willie are definitely from
the upper middle class. She sat on the knees of a future
archbishop, Charlie Hunter, when young, went to balls, and
drank "pink fizz" from "flute glasses" at her wedding.
When Willie appears downstage, he is *"dressed to kill —
top hat, morning coat, striped trousers, etc. Very long
bushy white Battle of Britain moustache."* Quite possibly he
was a colonel.

With *How It Is* and *Play* we are once more in an indefinite future, this time beyond the grave in hell or purgatory.
The characters, however, remember fragments of their life
"in the light" when they had a civil status — in fact, their
memories are part of their punishment. The two women
and the man in *Play* lived in the suburbs — evoked, for instance, by the sound of a lawn-mower — and could afford to
close up their houses and go abroad. The narrator's "images" in *How It Is* often have a startling immediacy; here is
one:

> next another image yet another so soon again the third
> perhaps they'll soon cease it's me all of me and my

mother's face I see it from below it's like nothing I ever saw

We are on a veranda smothered in verbena the scented sun dapples the red tiles yes I assure you

the huge head hatted with birds and flowers is bowed down over my curls the eyes burn with severe love I offer her mine pale upcast to the sky whence cometh our help* and which I know perhaps even then with time shall pass away

in a word bolt upright on a cushion on my knees whelmed in a nightshirt I pray according to her instructions that's not all she closes her eyes and drones a snatch of the so-called Apostles' Creed I steal a look at her lips

She stops her eyes burn down on me again I cast up mine in haste and repeat awry

The air thrills with the hum of insects that's all it goes out like a lamp blown out

This haunting passage is clearly based upon the famous photograph of Beckett at the age of four kneeling with bowed head at his mother's knee while she holds his clasped hands in her right hand.[5] The picture was taken for the benefit of his Aunt "Cissie" Beckett, who wanted to use it as a model for a painting. The unnamed narrator may therefore be thought of as having had a childhood and a social status similar to those of his creator.

Other, earlier characters of whom this may be true are Malone and one of the characters he "invents," Lemuel, whose name plainly suggests Samuel. Malone writes:

* A favorite Beckett misquotation for "I will lift up mine eyes unto the hills, from whence cometh our help."

> I was present at one of the first loopings of the loop, so
> help me God. I was not afraid. It was above a race-
> course, my mother held me by the hand. She kept say-
> ing, It's a miracle, a miracle.

This suggests both Leopardstown Racecourse and the piety
of Beckett's own mother. Lying in bed in boyhood, "in
the house in the plain," Malone hears much that Beckett
must have heard, including "the barking of the dogs, at
night . . . up in the hills, where the stone-cutters
lived. . . ." The murderous Lemuel, just before he runs
amok,

> watches the mountains rising behind the steeples be-
> yond the harbour, no they are no more
>
> No, they are no more than hills, they raise themselves
> gently, faintly blue, out of the confused plain. It was
> there somewhere he was born, in a fine house, of loving
> parents. Their slopes are covered with ling and furze, its
> hot yellow bells, better known as gorse. The hammers
> of the stone-cutters ring all day like bells.

No Dubliner can fail to evoke, as he reads this prose poem,
the steeples beyond Dún Laoire harbour, and the so-called
Dublin Mountains, indeed no more than hills, with stone-
quarries in their slopes.

How does it come about, though, this *dégringolade*, this
tumble down the social scale from gentleman to tramp?
Not, certainly, in the approved Victorian way — drink,
women, gambling. Beckett's tramp characters are ascetics
who barely eat, let alone drink, and may remain virgin, like
Macmann of *Malone Dies*, until their eighties. (When it is
suggested that drink was Watt's downfall, Mr. Nixon says,
"Oh my goodness no, . . . he drinks nothing but milk.")

Having no money, they never gamble. If they have lost all status and even shelter, it is because, like Victor in *Eleuthéria*, they have turned their backs on the world. They have made *il gran rifiuto*, the great refusal, in a way that even Dante might have approved of. Unlike hermits or mystics, however, they have not made this renunciation in the name of any spiritual truth. They are usually very unhappy and long for death.

Sometimes, perhaps, their fall is involuntary. Of the "Notes" appended to *Film*, No. 13 describes the photographs torn up by O, seven in all. The first two of these show

> 1. Male infant. Six months. His mother holds him in her arms. Infant smiles front. Mother's big hands. Her severe eyes devouring him. Her big old-fashioned be-flowered hat.

> 2. The same. Four years. On a veranda, dressed in loose nightshirt, kneeling on a cushion, attitude of prayer, hands clasped, head bowed, eyes closed. Half profile. Mother on chair beside him, big hands on knees, head bowed towards him, severe eyes, similar hat to 1.

The second of these offers a more accurate description than the passage in *How It Is* of the famous photograph, a copy of which was in fact momentarily visible in the film. No. 3 is the same boy at fifteen, in a school blazer, teaching a dog to beg. Next he is graduating from college at twenty; at twenty-one he has his arm round his fiancée; at twenty-five, bareheaded, moustached, newly enlisted, he stands in uniform, holding a little girl in his arms. The last of these seven ages shows "The same. 30 years. Looking over 40. Wearing hat and overcoat. Patch over left eye. Clean-shaven. Grim expression." We hardly need to know any more about what has happened to him in the last five years. War has taken much more from him than the sight of one eye. The stony features of Buster Keaton, star of *Film*, are wholly appropriate to this snapshot.

Part II of *Molloy* describes another way of divesting oneself of a bourgeois identity: Moran, in effect, kills himself. The resulting liberation produces some of the most euphoric passages in Beckett's entire *œuvre*. Even before the symbolic killing, Moran had become conscious of "my growing resignation to being dispossessed of self." The onset of lameness in one leg had already made him aware that "when of the innumerable attitudes adopted unthinkingly by the normal man all are precluded but two or three, then these are enhanced." Perhaps "the great classical paralyses" would "offer . . . even still more unspeakable satisfactions." The man whom Moran kills is dressed differently from himself: instead of Moran's straw boater and "old pepper-and-salt shooting-suit with the knee-breeches,"

> He wore a thick navy-blue suit (double-breasted) of hideous cut and a pair of outrageously wide black shoes. . . . He had a narrow-brimmed dark blue felt hat on his head, with a fish-hook and an artificial fly stuck in the band, which produced a highly sporting effect.

These unattractive details were as nothing "compared to the face which I regret to say vaguely resembled my own, less the refinement of course, same little abortive moustache, same little ferrety eyes, same paraphimosis of the nose, and a thin red mouth that looked as if it was raw from trying to shit its tongue."

Soon this unprepossessing "stranger" is found by Moran "stretched on the ground, his head in a pulp. . . . He no longer resembled me." Not long after this, Moran is as helpless and deprived as the Molloy he set out to find. But he seems content. Having returned to his dilapidated house and having written his report on his fruitless search for Molloy, he tells us:

> I am clearing out. Perhaps I shall meet Molloy. My knee is no better. It is no worse either. I have crutches now. I shall go faster, all will go faster. They will be happy days. I shall learn. All there was to sell I have sold. But I had heavy debts. I have been a man long enough, I shall not put up with it any more, I shall not try any more.

Moran cannot remember the actual process that led to the death of the man who resembled him; he may not even have been the murderer. Yet the death of this man undoubtedly symbolizes the annihilation of the self, which paradoxically is also a realization of the self. Even before this murderous encounter Moran seemed to see "a frenzied collapsing of all that had always protected me from all I was always condemned to be." It is true that for a time after the man's death Moran continues to resemble his old self, tyrannizing over his son until the boy robs him and runs away, leaving him "alone, with my bag, my umbrella . . . and fifteen shillings. . . ." After that, however, as he limps home day after day, he becomes conscious of how much (and how little) he has changed:

> Physically speaking it seemed to me I was now becoming rapidly unrecognizable. And when I passed my hands over my face, . . . the face my hands felt was

not my face any more, and the hands my face felt were
my hands no longer. And yet the gist of the sensation
was the same as in the far-off days when I was well-
shaven and perfumed and proud of my intellectual's
soft white hands. And this belly I did not know remained my belly, my old belly, thanks to I know not
what intuition. And to tell the truth I not only knew
who I was, but I had a sharper and clearer sense of my
identity than ever before. . . .

Thus, although Moran takes upon him the lameness and
destitution that we have come to associate with Molloy, he
still retains his identity. He has escaped from the rigidities
— social, occupational, religious — that penned in his true
self, perhaps. Yet now he hears "a voice telling me things.
. . . It told me to write the report. Does this mean I am
freer now than I was? I do not know. I shall learn. Then I
went back into the house and wrote, It is midnight. The
rain is beating on the windows. It was not midnight. It was
not raining."

What do these last sentences of Moran and of the entire
novel *Molloy* mean? Has everything in his "report" been
untrue? Has he made up all his adventures in order to create a new Moran in imagination only? Are we to give an
affirmative answer to the question about his greater freedom? Does the writing of fiction permit the author to escape himself? The whole thrust of Beckett's next novel,
Malone Dies, denies this. While waiting for his imminent
death, Malone plans to play, to tell himself stories. He begins a story about a young man, Saposcat, but soon he is
wondering "if I am not talking yet again about myself." A
little farther on, he takes heart: "We are getting on. Nothing is less like me than this patient, reasonable child. . . .

If this continues it is myself I shall lose and the thousand ways that lead there. . . . and on the threshold of being no more I succeed in being another." But he loses interest in the story and writes more and more about his present state. Then, pulling himself together, he expresses his first intention more pessimistically: "Yes, a little creature, I shall try and make a little creature, to hold in my arms, a little creature in my image, no matter what I say. And seeing what a poor thing I have made, or how like myself, I shall eat it." (The Joycean idea of the artist as god has been given an ironic twist here.)

Malone returns to the story of "Sapo" on the next page, but he now calls him Macmann and describes him as old, destitute and for a time as crippled as Malone himself. Eventually Macmann finds himself in "a kind of asylum. . . . the House of Saint John of God. . . ." There, like Malone, he is taken care of at first by an old woman, though Malone claims to be certain that his own room "is not a room in a hospital or a madhouse." Later, Macmann is transferred to the care of Lemuel, who has had a boyhood rather similar, as we have seen, to both Malone's and Beckett's. As the novel ends, Lemuel runs amok and Malone dies.

> Lemuel is in charge, he raises his hatchet on which the blood will never dry, but not to hit anyone, he will not hit anyone, he will not hit anyone any more, he will not touch anyone any more, either with it or with it or with it or with
>
> or with it or with his hammer or with his stick or with his fist or in thought in dream I mean never he will never

or with his pencil or with his stick or

Malone, we remember, has a club in his room somewhere.
"It is stained with blood, but insufficiently, insufficiently."
The author, then, inevitably writes about himself: this is as
true of Beckett as it is of Malone. Has Beckett therefore
committed murder? Yes, as we all have, "in thought in
dream . . . or with his pencil. . . ."

Earlier, Malone / Beckett has explained this with only a
little ambiguity:

> But let us leave these morbid matters and get on with
> that of my demise, in two or three days if I remember
> rightly. Then it will be all over with the Murphys, Mer-
> ciers, Molloys, Morans and Malones, unless it goes on
> beyond the grave [in *How It Is*, perhaps]. But sufficient
> unto the day, let us first defunge, then we'll see. How
> many have I killed, hitting them on the head or setting
> fire to them? Off-hand I can only think of four, all un-
> knowns, I never knew anyone. A sudden wish, I have a
> sudden wish to see, as sometimes in the old days, some-
> thing, anything, no matter what, something I could
> not have imagined. There was the old butler too, in Lon-
> don I think, . . . I cut his throat with a razor, that
> makes five.

The old butler slit his own throat, actually, in *Murphy*.
The other dead are probably Belacqua (who died under
anaesthesia), Murphy (set fire to), the charcoal-burner
struck down by Molloy, the man killed by Moran. Beckett
may have forgotten the policeman murdered by Mercier
and Camier or omitted him because *Mercier et Camier*
had not yet been published. All these shapes of death, however, have one thing in common — they are imagined. In

this dimension at any rate, Beckett is unlikely to see something that he could not have imagined. But what about images of beauty and joy, can he not see these too? As a man, perhaps, but not as a writer: he cannot imagine them and therefore he cannot see them in such a way as to make us see them.

It has been suggested that Beckett's preoccupation with tramps began after he was stabbed in the chest by a Paris *clochard* on 7 January 1938. When asked why he had attacked Beckett, the man said he did not know. We are invited to read *Molloy*, for example, as Beckett / Moran seeking identity with *clochard* / Molloy; but it has become clear from a close reading that Moran, far from losing his identity, has had his sense of it sharpened and clarified. Beckett, like Malone, has sought unceasingly to divest himself of his identity by means of his art, but in the end he remains what he always was, an Irish gentleman of the professional classes, reared by a sporting father and an evangelical mother. In his personal life he is incapable of being rude, unkind, self-seeking or aggressive; if we are to believe his most intimate poetry, he also reproaches himself with a corresponding incapacity to love. For all his quiet pessimism, there may be more of the Beckett his friends and acquaintances know in Winnie of *Happy Days* than in many of his other characters. In broad self-caricature he resembles the one male character of *Play*, who, even in hell or purgatory, cannot refrain from saying "Pardon" every time he hiccups. But most of all he resembles Listener in *That Time* (1976).

In any case, it is not quite true to say that Watt was the first of Beckett's tramps. There is the tinker in "Walking

Out," for instance, who remains "devoid of rancour" when Belacqua's bitch urinates over his trousers:

> "Wettin me throusers" said the vagabond mildly "wuss 'n meself."

There is the pedlar in "Ding-Dong," who sells "seats in heaven . . . tuppence apiece, four fer a tanner.". Characteristically, "her speech was that of a woman of the people, but of a gentlewoman of the people." Belacqua himself, when he vomits over the boots of a Civic Guard in "A Wet Night" and then falls to his knees in the vomit, becomes as abject a figure in his drunkenness as any of his successors do in sobriety. As for Cooper in *Murphy*, in spite of his alcoholism and the energy which earns him the description of a "ruthless tout," he is in some ways a first sketch for Watt, Molloy, Malone and, indeed, O in *Film:*

> He was a low-sized, clean-shaven, gray-faced, one-eyed man, triorchous and a non-smoker. He had a curious hunted walk, like that of a destitute diabetic in a strange city. He never sat down and never took off his hat.

When, after the death of Murphy, he feels free of these twin compulsions and celebrates by sitting down on his hat, this turns out, unsurprisingly, to be an "ancient bowler."

I began this chapter with a comment on style; it will be appropriate to end it with another. Despite the obscenities and other colloquial or slang phrases that startle us on first acquaintance with *Molloy, Malone Dies* and *Waiting for Godot,* the best confirmation of my thesis that the protagonists are *personae* of their creator will be found in the astonishing nobility of much of their language. It should be added, in view of one example cited just below, that obscenity and slang are not confined to the French: in many cases the English translation is more colloquial or more obscene than the original.* Examples of noble style are equally common in both languages. I use the word "noble" rather than "grand" because nobility is compatible with ugliness, weakness and pathos. I use it in the sense in which it is applied by Moran to the man with the big stick: "His face was dirty and hairy, yes, pale, noble, dirty and hairy."

Molloy begins in a style of misleading simplicity:

> Je suis dans la chambre de ma mère. C'est moi qui y vis maintenant.

> (I am in my mother's room. It's I who live there now.)

Not much more than twenty pages has gone by, however, when we come on the following passage, in which Molloy regrets that he has never learned "the guiding principles of good manners";

> Car cela m'aurait permis, avant d'étaler en public certaines façons de faire relevant de la seule commodité du corps, tels le doigt dans le nez, la main sous les couilles, le mouchage sans mouchoir et la pissade ambulante, de m'en référer aux premières règles d'une théorie raisonnée. Oui, je n'avais à ce sujet que des notions négatives et empiriques. . . .

> (For that would have allowed me, before parading in public certain habits such as the finger in the nose, the

* There are several notable examples near the end of *Malone Dies*: "shit and misery" (a Portora phrase in my day) for *saloperies et pourritures*; "you old whore" for *charogne*; "but to hell with all this fucking scenery" for *mais il s'agit bien de la nature*; "Fuck off" for *La paix*.

scratching of the balls, digital emunction and the peri-
patetic piss, to refer them to the first rules of a reasoned
theory. On this subject I had only negative and empiri-
cal notions.)

The phrase *relevant de la seule commodité du corps* has
been omitted, but the English translation, "by Patrick
Bowles in collaboration with the author," is otherwise
faithful to the drily pedantic tone of the original, which
rather resembles that of the narrative voice in *Murphy*.
Molloy is far from being the simple child of nature that his
bodily habits suggest. A moment later he achieves, in both
the French and the English, that noble style I am seeking
to exemplify:

> Mais c'est seulement depuis que je ne vis plus que je
> pense, à ces choses-là et aux autres. C'est dans la tran-
> quillité de la décomposition que je me rappelle cette
> longue émotion confuse que fut ma vie, et que je la
> juge, comme il est dit que Dieu nous jugera et avec
> autant d'impertinence.

> (But it is only since I have ceased to live that I think of
> these things and the other things. It is in the tranquil-
> lity of decomposition that I remember the long con-
> fused emotion which was my life, and that I judge it, as
> it is said that God will judge me, and with no less
> impertinence.)

The second sentence in the French is worthy of Pascal, except of course for that final impertinent phrase, *et avec
autant d'impertinence*, which, though not violating the
Pascalian prose rhythm, does give an un-Pascalian twist to
the thought. The piety of *Dieu nous jugera* (God will judge
us) is already diminished in the English by the change to

"God will judge me," lessening the shock of "and with no less impertinence."

Many of the instances of a noble style in *Malone Dies* may be misleading: when Malone writes about Saposcat / Macmann, he frequently verges on parody or pastiche of the traditional novel or biography, and indeed becomes aware of this at times; nevertheless, he presses on:

> Sapo loved nature, took an interest
> This is awful.
>
> Sapo loved nature, took an interest in animals and plants and willingly raised his eyes to the sky, day and night. But he did not know how to look at all these things. . . . He did not associate the crocus with the spring nor the chrysanthemum with Michaelmas. The sun, the moon, the planets and the stars did not fill him with wonder. . . . But he loved the flight of the hawk and could distinguish it from all others. He would stand rapt, gazing at the long pernings, the quivering poise, the wings lifted for the plummet drop, the wild reascent, fascinated by such extremes of need, of pride, of patience and solitude.

Since Beckett himself translated *Malone meurt*, there is less need to consult the French, but let us note that it contains no true equivalent of the Yeatsian "pernings." The sentence in French begins, "Immobile il suivait des yeux les longs vols planés, . . ." If a model for Beckett's French in this passage were found, it would undoubtedly come from the Romantic period or later. The sentences with which Malone introduces Moll, on the other hand, might have been written by almost any incompetent nineteenth-century novelist: "She was a little old woman, immoderately ill-favoured of both face and body. She seems called on to play a certain part in the remarkable events which, I hope, will enable me to make an end." Nevertheless, when Malone writes in his own person about himself, he is capable of producing a brief prose poem worthy of Jules Laforgue:

> Weary with my weariness, white last moon, sole regret, not even. To be dead, before her, on her, with her, and turn, dead on dead, about poor mankind, and never have to die any more, from among the living. Not even, not even that. My moon was here below, far below, the little I was able to desire. And one day soon, soon, one earthlit night, beneath the earth, a dying being will say, like me, in the earthlight, Not even, not even that, and die, without having been able to find a regret.

This passage, like others in *Malone Dies*, is worthy to stand beside the already classic duet between Didi and Gogo in Act II of *Waiting for Godot* that begins with "All the dead voices. . . ." Since it is quoted in French in Chapter 6 below, I will not include it here. (The English text has been set to music by Marc Wilkinson.)[6] The tramp may be an ex-gentleman, an ex-scholar, but he never ceases to be a poet.

The reader must often have felt that my sociological approach in this chapter involves a curiously narrow reading of what are felt to be some of the most purely imaginative works of our generation. Often I have given a literal and humorless interpretation to words that were almost certainly written in jest. And yet the facts that Beckett gives free rein to his imagination and has insisted that he writes "in a trance" imply that he has the capacity to reveal the unconscious hopes and fears not only of himself

but of his social group. The Irish Protestant of the professional classes, like his Catholic counterpart, is not altogether imbued with what American sociologists like to call
"the Protestant ethic." He aspires to become a gentleman
— in economic terms, a *rentier* who lives off the labor of
others — but he fears to become a tramp. There are few
urban workers or peasants in Beckett's novels and almost
none in his plays. If he doesn't have an unearned income
and fails to establish himself in a profession, the Beckett
character never looks forward to a lifetime of "honest toil."
He becomes a parasite or a tramp. This is realistic: in Lein-
ster, Munster and Connacht the "poor Protestant" was a
rare bird in Beckett's youth and, where he existed, was liable
to the contempt of Protestant and Catholic alike. No wonder the Saposcat family were in such a fever of anxiety as
their son took his university entrance examination:

> The decisive moment was at hand when the hopes re-
> posed in Sapo were to be fulfilled, or dashed to the
> ground. . . . Mrs. Saposcat, whose piety grew warm in
> times of crisis, prayed for his success. Kneeling at her
> bedside, in her night-dress, she ejaculated, silently, for
> her husband would not have approved, Oh God grant
> he pass, grant he pass, grant he scrape through!
>
> When this first ordeal was surmounted there would
> be others. . . . But it seemed to the Saposcats that
> these would be less terrible than the first which was to
> give them, or deny them, the right to say, He is doing
> his medicine, or, He is reading for the bar. For they felt
> that a more or less normal if unintelligent youth, once
> admitted to the study of these professions, was almost
> sure to be certified, sooner or later, apt to exercise them.
> For they had experience of doctors, and of lawyers, like
> most people.

There is the bourgeois nightmare at its worst — all the more intensely traumatic because it is stated so baldly and briefly.

J. M. Synge, who came out of an Irish Protestant family very similar to Beckett's, explicitly stated that the artist in a middle-class family possesses the same temperament that would have made him a tramp if his parents were small farmers. It is fairly clear that Synge thought his own family, in their less charitable moments, viewed him as little better than a tramp. Though Beckett the man never had the instincts of a "hippie," his creative self has toyed with all the possibilities of the tramp. Moran sees the tramp as a free man — the process of his destitution becoming the stages of his liberation — a romantic view that Synge often shared. Much of Molloy's and Watt's experience shows us the tramp as victim. Malone is an example of the tramp presented quite literally as an artist — a novelist. Vladimir and Estragon represent the comic, Chaplinesque tramp who is at once clown and philosopher. Most extraordinary of all, the protagonist of *How It Is* offers the mirror-image of the tramp as victim: he is the tramp as executioner, as tyrant, as sadist. But always, at the back of our minds and of Beckett's too, there is the image of the tramp as scapegoat, the tramp as an ironic, half-involuntary Christ.

VLADIMIR   But you can't go barefoot!
ESTRAGON   Christ did.
VLADIMIR   Christ! What has Christ got to do with it? You're not going to compare yourself to Christ!
ESTRAGON   All my life I've compared myself to him.
VLADIMIR   But where he lived it was warm, it was dry!
ESTRAGON   Yes. And they crucified quick.
            Silence.

4

CLASSICISM / ABSURDISM

The dialectic always present in Beckett's art has been neglected by most critics who have analyzed the *form* of his plays. As to the *content*, few intelligent students have been misled: they have seen the compassion as well as the cruelty, the comedy as well as the pathos, the beauty as well as the ugliness. What they have too often failed to see, in their eagerness to proclaim the "absurdist" irrationality of dialogue and action, is the classical, logical structure present in every one of Beckett's dramatic works. Worse still, in their anxiety to recognize the avant-garde novelties of Beckett's theater, they have failed to notice his revival of some ancient stage conventions that had long fallen into disuse. I am not now referring to the conventions of the circus, the music-hall, or even the *commedia dell'arte* — all of which have already been recognized in Beckett's stage plays — but to those of a much more sophisticated dramatic tradition.

"All creativity consists in making something out of nothing. . . . ("Toute l'invention consiste à faire quelque chose de rien. . . .") This quotation from Racine's preface to his tragedy *Bérénice,* in which nothing happens for five acts, could also serve as a defense of, say, *Waiting for Godot,* "a play in which nothing happens, *twice.*"[1] Every Beckett critic would profit by reading the entire preface and also Racine's first preface to *Britannicus,* in which he rebukes his critics for not being satisfied with "a single action, not overloaded with matter . . ." ("une action simple, chargée de peu de matière. . . ."). They had apparently been complaining, like Estragon in *Waiting for Godot* and many in that play's first American audience, "Nothing happens, nobody comes, nobody goes, it's awful!" Racine went on to sneer at them for expecting him to cram into "an action that takes place in a single day" a quantity of incidents that would take a month to happen.

Although Beckett has never taken on his detractors directly in the brash manner of Racine, I think it is no accident that Racine's arguments provide such a strong defense of Beckett's dramaturgy. On the one hand, Beckett's supposedly avant-garde plays observe many of the rules for neoclassical tragedy; on the other hand, Beckett has studied the work of Racine more closely than that of any other dramatist, Shakespeare included. He may not have taken the French poet to his heart as he did Dante, whose cosmogony and characters — especially Belacqua, of course — permeate the Beckett world, but Racine's tragedies were an inescapable fact of his education, as of mine. Nobody who took the French honors course at Trinity College, Dublin, under Professor T. B. Rudmose-Brown could safely avoid reading not merely all the eleven tragedies of Racine but also his only comedy, *Les Plaideurs*.

Beckett's great admiration for Rudmose-Brown has already been referred to in Chapter 2: he would have found little difficulty in sharing his professor's liking for Racine and his distaste for Corneille. The first dramatic work by Beckett in any language was *Le Kid* (1931), a parody of Corneille's *Le Cid*, written in French in collaboration with Georges Pelorson, a successor of Alfred Péron as exchange lecturer in French at Trinity. When *Le Kid* was performed by the Dublin University Modern Language Society at the Peacock Theatre, Beckett held the Trinity post of Assistant in French. Rudmose-Brown thought so highly of his assistant that he allowed him to lecture on Racine, a pleasure that he later used to reserve for himself. At least one set of notes on Beckett's lectures still exists, kept by his pupil Rachel Dobbin, now better known as an actress in Dublin under her married name of Rachel Burrows. Her notebook shows that in his last term at Trinity (Michaelmas 1931) Beckett concentrated on *Andromaque*, *Phèdre*, and *Bérénice*, but referred also to *Athalie*, *Britannicus* and *Bajazet* in his lectures on Racine.

Beckett's neo-classicism has escaped the notice of most French critics, as well as of most English-speaking scholars studying French literature, though Wallace Fowlie observed in 1959 that *Godot* possesses an "utter simplicity" in the classical French tradition. Still, one French critic, Georges Belmont,* headed his review of the original pro-

---

* The index to Federman and Fletcher's *Samuel Beckett: His Works and His Critics* points out that Georges Belmont is the pseudonym of Georges Pelorson, co-author of *Le Kid*.

duction of *Godot* "Un classicisme retrouvé" and remarked that "the three unities are not so much observed in it as pitilessly present."[2] One could argue that the unity of action is broken by the irruption of Pozzo and Lucky into each act, but, since Pozzo is at first mistaken for Godot, this argument is not entirely valid. Actually, I hold the view that Pozzo *is* Godot; on this interpretation, the play becomes almost too tightly knit. Beckett's next stage play, *Endgame*, consisting of one long act, observes the three unities of time, place and action with even greater rigor. Now that sets are expensive, it's natural enough for two-acters like *Godot* and *Happy Days* to be played in a single set, but even these two plays come close to observing the least respected unity, that of time; following Aristotle's suggestion, *Godot* certainly "tries as far as possible to keep within a single revolution of the sun, or only slightly to exceed it," its action taking place on two successive evenings. In *Happy Days* the sun no longer even *seems* to move, but if we speak in "the old style," as Winnie habitually does, then the play's action occurs during part of two possibly successive "days." Not only is the unity of place rigorously observed in all Beckett's stage plays, but, true to the rules of Racinian tragedy, the scene is always a *lieu vague*, neither here nor there: "A country road. A tree." The setting of *Bérénice*, for example, may seem quite specific at first, but it is in truth a no-man's-land: "The scene is at Rome, in a room between the apartment of Titus and that of Bérénice."

It is a commonplace of Beckett criticism that his characters come in pairs, especially on the stage: Didi and Gogo, Pozzo and Lucky, Hamm and Clov, Nagg and Nell; but

Racine's characters too come in pairs. Look at the *dramatis personae* of *Bérénice*, for instance. (It will soon become clear why I refer so often to this tragedy.) Titus has Paulin for his *confident*, Antiochus has Arsace for his, and Bérénice's *confidente* is Phénice; the only other character is a messenger, Rutile, just as the only unpaired character in *Godot* is the Boy who serves as messenger in both acts. Racine finds the device of the *confident* indispensable for his kind of psychological drama: without it, his plays would consist almost entirely of soliloquies. Very often, the *confident* or *confidente* personifies the main character's better or worse self: Oenone, for example, persuades Phèdre to reveal her love for her stepson Hippolyte. Beckett employs his paired characters for a similar purpose, though he is not afraid to create short works like *Not I* and *Eh Joe* that consist entirely of monologue; *Krapp's Last Tape* is a special case, since we hear the thirty-nine-year-old Krapp on tape as well as seeing and hearing his present self, thirty years older. In *Endgame*, Clov asks, "What is there to keep me here?" "The dialogue," replies Hamm. A literal translation of the original French is more pointed: "What use am I?" "You give me my cue." Hamm soliloquizes a great deal, in fact, but it was not until *Happy Days* that Beckett discovered how to write a longish play consisting almost entirely of monologue. By establishing the taciturn Willie from the start as a virtually unseen and unheard *confident*, he made Winnie's constant stream of chatter plausible.

Why did Beckett employ these archaic conventions so consistently? I think the answer must be that they were the only conventions he knew for a non-realist drama. He told me in 1956 that before writing *Godot* he had never been a keen theatergoer, except for "about a year" in his student days, when he attended every revival and new production staged at the Abbey Theatre. However, the plays he remembers having seen at the Abbey — listed in Chapter 2 — suggest that he visited the theater at least sporadically throughout the years 1924-27. For example, the two Lennox Robinson plays he named had their first productions in April 1924 and October 1925. Yeats's *Oedipus the King* and *Oedipus at Colonus* were first performed in December 1926 and September 1927, respectively. *Fanny's First Play*, by Shaw, was first staged by the Abbey in April 1925, though written over a decade earlier. Although O'Casey's early plays were frequently revived, it is possible that Beckett saw the first production of *Juno and the Paycock* in March 1924 and that of *The Plough and the Stars* in February 1926. What he learned from Robinson and O'Casey can be seen in *All That Fall*, in *The Old Tune*, and perhaps even in the surprisingly realistic dialogue of *Play*, a work not entirely beyond Lennox Robinson's capacity. Nevertheless, Sophocles as transmitted by Yeats was much more relevant to, for example, *Endgame* than the Abbey version of realism, even though Synge's plays, among others, tended to burst the bonds imposed by a realist convention. Beckett followed the honors course in English for some time and occasionally quotes Shakespeare in his works, but instead of using any English dramatist, even the greatest, as a model he turned — perhaps quite unconsciously — to Racine.

Those who think of Racine as the supreme dramatist of hopeless, self-destructive passion and ruthless ambition may well wonder where anything of the kind is to be found in Beckett. My answer is that it first appears in a novel, sev-

eral years before Beckett began to write serious plays. Early
in *Murphy* there occurs a sort of parody of a Racine plot —
that of *Andromaque*, say, where Oreste loves Hermione,
who loves Pyrrhus, who loves Andromaque, who loves her
dead husband, Hector. In her notes on Beckett's discussion
of *Andromaque*, Mrs. Burrows wrote and underlined the
words "*Situation circle*" opposite an outline of the plot
similar to the one just given. The situation in *Murphy* actually forms a perfect circle, beginning with "Neary's love
for Miss Dwyer, who loved a Flight-Lieutenant Elliman,
who loved a Miss Farren of Ringaskiddy, who loved a Father Fitt of Ballinclashet, who in all sincerity was bound to
acknowledge a certain vocation for a Mrs. West of Passage,
who loved Neary." Later, the susceptible Neary falls hopelessly in love with Miss Counihan, who loves Murphy, who
loves Celia. As sometimes happens in Racine's plays, Celia
in turn loves Murphy, but this does not prevent disaster.
Murphy's duty, as the world sees it, is to keep Celia off the
streets by taking a job; but the only job he can get keeps
him away from Celia and ends in his being burned to death.
Besides the parody, then, *Murphy* contains a fairly serious
Racine-style plot.

Krapp's Last Tape also concerns a hopeless love: "I said
again I thought it was hopeless and no good going on and
she agreed. . . ." There may even be a conflict between
love and ambition, implied in the last words of the play,
from the tape made by Krapp on his thirty-ninth birthday:
"Perhaps my best years are gone. When there was a chance
of happiness. But I wouldn't want them back. Not with the
fire in me now. No, I wouldn't want them back." The older
Krapp who listens to these words thinks his younger self

was a "stupid bastard." The "fire" is dead, the *opus magnum* has been completed — net sale, seventeen copies — but the love affair that he thought was hopeless, and perhaps gave up for the sake of his great work, still haunts him. "The eyes she had!"

Beckett's most Racinian play is entitled, with classical simplicity, *Play*. It can be found in embryo in the following passage from *Murphy*, which deals with the brief love-life of a grotesque minor character, the one-eyed, three-testicled Cooper: ". . . of the only two good angels he had ever been able to care for, simultaneously as ill luck would have it, the one, a Miss A, then a brunette, was now in her seventeenth year of His Majesty's pleasure, while the other, a Miss B, also formerly a brunette, had not yet succumbed to her injuries." Twenty-five years later, *Play* used the same plot, shorn of its melodramatic attempted murder but set in a sort of purgatory where two women and a man, each encased to the neck in an urn, are forced to recapitulate their brief mutual entanglement; none is aware of the presence of the other two. First Woman thinks that Man ran away with Second Woman, but the latter in fact went away alone and thinks that Man and First Woman are still together. Man knows he ran away from both, though he wanted to remain the lover of both. The whole situation resembles very closely that of *Bérénice*, in which two men, the Emperor Titus and King Antiochus, are in love with the heroine; Bérénice, for her part, is in love with Titus and regards Antiochus as her dearest friend. Yet the tragedy ends, bloodlessly, with Titus remaining unwillingly in Rome, while the other two reluctantly leave the city to go their separate ways. By the end of *Bérénice*, all three major characters have threatened to commit suicide; perhaps the three characters in *Play* are being punished because they *have* committed suicide.

If *Play* is Beckett at his most Racinian, *Bérénice* is Racine at his most Beckettian: as I have said, he makes something out of nothing for five acts, while keeping a sympathetic audience riveted to their seats. The chief reason why one says that nothing happens in *Bérénice* or *Endgame* or *Waiting for Godot* is that the situation at the end remains exactly the same as at the beginning. Possible resolutions of the deadlock are suggested, but by the end of the play all of them have been rejected. Gogo begins *Waiting for Godot* with the words "Nothing to be done." Soon, we learn that he and Didi are waiting for Godot. At the end of two acts, Gogo says, "I can't go on like this," but they are still waiting. *Endgame* could equally well have been entitled "Stalemate." Hamm assumes at the end the exact posture we found him in at the beginning. The situation cannot be resolved: if Clov leaves the refuge, he must die, and the helpless Hamm will die too. If Clov stays, they will both die anyway, though a little later. Bérénice actually does leave Rome, but that decisive step does not make her own life, or the lives of the two men who love her, any less unbearable. This fact alone would be sufficient to justify Racine's calling his bloodless drama a tragedy. Nevertheless, the Beckett of 1931 told his students to consider *Bérénice* a comedy: it had, he said, a comic resolution, the establishment of equilibrium, whereas a tragic resolution involved the "abolition of any need of equilibrium." For him, the comic spirit as seen in Molière was an "oscillation between equilibrium and lack of it"; the tragic spirit required "progression from complexity to integrity."

Lucien Goldmann, however, in his *Racine* offers a definition of tragedy as *"any play in which the conflicts are necessarily insoluble,"*[3] a description that applies not only to Beckett's stage plays but to much of his dramatic work for other media, including *Embers, Eh Joe* and *Film*. Goldmann was clearly trying to create an image of Racine that would appeal to the second half of the twentieth century, and it must be agreed that he succeeded: almost every page of the book makes one think of Beckett, although Goldmann doesn't mention him even once. Adhering to his own definition, Goldmann regards only three of Racine's plays — *Britannicus, Bérénice* and *Phèdre* — as tragedies in the fullest sense; *Andromaque* is tragic "up to a certain point," but the rest of Racine and of course all of Corneille's so-called tragedies are classified as "dramas."[4] Goldmann connects Racine's four true tragedies with the doctrine of "extremist Jansenism," according to which God is hidden, "so hidden that it is impossible to know his will" or to have "the slightest indication of whether we are damned or saved."[5] This has been regarded by some critics as also the theme of *Waiting for Godot.** The related question "What must we do to be saved?" of course becomes unanswerable: it is dramatized in *Play* as the three characters try to discover what will save them from the pitiless interrogation of the spotlight.

In one respect, however, Beckett has made a technical advance beyond Racine, creating a dramatic structure even

---

* Pascal is, of course, the most famous literary exponent of *le dieu caché*.

more rigidly perfect than that arrived at in *Bérénice*. Just before the end of *Play* we read the stage direction "*Repeat play exactly.*" After this repeat has been completed, the actors return yet again to the speeches with which *Play* began, indicating that the whole cycle is about to be run through once more; the fall of the curtain mercifully cuts them off. The return to the initial situation that we have noted in *Endgame* and both acts of *Waiting for Godot* already implied the circularity of form that *Play* was to make explicit; indeed it had been made explicit earlier in a minor work, *Act Without Words II*. *Happy Days*, like *Waiting for Godot*, can be described as two circular acts, the second of which recapitulates most of the material presented in the first. Act II of *Happy Days*, however, omits more material and recapitulates the rest more briefly than the second act of *Godot*, suggesting Beckett's greater command of his medium in the later work. (One has to acknowledge, though, that Winnie without arms naturally finds fewer things to do than when her arms and hands were still unburied.) While *Endgame* and *Godot* end in stasis, *Happy Days* concludes with a *coup de théâtre* — the appearance of Willie in full evening-dress and top-hat. A new situation has been reached, making the end of this play unique in the Beckett canon.*

The works for media other than the stage show a linear rather than a circular form, but every Beckett stage play reveals some circularity to a diligent searcher. For instance, *Not I* can be interpreted as a one-character version of *Play*: Mouth has already repeated certain phrases several times before the curtain falls, especially the key phrase "what?

* See pp. 221-23 below.

. . . who? . . . no! . . . she!" It begins to seem likely
that she will soon exhaust her repertoire and begin to repeat
it all word for word if the play lasts much longer. *Krapp's
Last Tape* at first seems reassuringly linear, moving forward
from snatches of an old tape made when Krapp was twenty-
seven or twenty-nine to Krapp's account of his thirty-ninth
year to Krapp recording himself at sixty-nine. But the crux
of the play, of course, is that Krapp keeps turning back to a
love scene described on the tape he made at age thirty-nine.
When the play ends, we have just heard part of that scene
for the third time, so that the form of the work may be
thought of as resembling a spiral rather than a circle.

In retrospect, it is easy to see why the absurdist label was
so mistakenly pinned to *Waiting for Godot* and then, inevitably, to the plays that followed. One of the chief reasons for this misunderstanding was, paradoxically, Beckett's
adoption or adaptation of neo-classical form. The French
drama critics were looking for a linear structure in *Godot*;
confronted instead with a circular one, they almost unani-
mously decided that there was no structure there at all. Accustomed on the whole to praise plays that were crowded
with action, they forgot Racine's admirable phrase about
making something out of nothing; they must even have forgotten Sartre's masterpiece, *Huis clos* (*No Exit*), in which,
once the three principal characters have arrived on stage,
nobody comes and nobody is allowed to go. I have often
wondered whether Beckett could ever have developed his
own special dramaturgy without the example of Sartre before him as well as that of Racine. *Godot, Endgame, Play*
are all offspring of *Huis clos*.

We cannot totally acquit Beckett of the charge that he

deliberately set out to mislead his audience. As we saw in the previous chapter, the seedy costumes and very colloquial — even at times obscene — dialogue of Vladimir and Estragon led people to mistake them for tramps. These features also led critics to mistake the dramatic convention in which the play is written: what they took for realism was in fact neo-classicism, as the noble diction of certain exchanges between the two principal characters eventually revealed. Still, it must be admitted that *Godot* is not a pure example of either dramatic convention. If Beckett was conscious of mixing his genres, he may have been trying to disorient his audience: at any rate, he succeded in doing so. All sorts of conventional assumptions — philosophic and social as well as artistic — were disturbed or overthrown by the play.

Furthermore, every member of the audience at the first performance of *En attendant Godot* must have been aware of a quality in the play that seems totally at variance with the classical: the air of improvisation. Alain Robbe-Grillet, although concerned to stress certain philosophic overtones, provides the best description of this quality:

> The dramatic character, in most cases, merely *plays a role*, like the people around us who evade their own existence. In Beckett's play, on the contrary, everything happens as if the two tramps were on stage *without having a role*.
>
> They *are there*; they must explain themselves. But they do not seem to have a text prepared beforehand and scrupulously learned by heart, to support them. They must invent. They are free.[6]

Sometimes, what they appear to invent looks highly original, but at other times, as when Didi and Gogo exchange hats, both their own and Lucky's, we recognize the pattern at once: it is a comic set-piece, known in English music-hall as a "turn," in American vaudeville as a "routine," in *commedia dell'arte* as a *lazzo*. Even if we are not familiar with a particular set-piece — for instance the attempt to hang themselves at the end of Act II — it may be as ancient as mime itself. If Beckett had read much of the early Dublin criticism of O'Casey's first plays, he must have been aware that those quite firmly constructed melodramas were frequently accused of being a mere succession of music-hall turns, including singers as well as patter and knockabout comedians. *Waiting for Godot* lies open to the same accusation; it even includes a song by Vladimir, in which incidentally the circular structure of *Play* is anticipated by several years:

> A dog came in the kitchen
> And stole a crust of bread.
> Then cook up with a ladle
> And beat him till he was dead.
>
> Then all the dogs came running
> and dug the dog a tomb
> And wrote upon the tombstone
> For the eyes of dogs to come:
>
> A dog came in the kitchen . . .

"Absurdity" in the philosophical sense implies irrationality, confusion, the absence of meaning and purpose. Beckett has often amused himself by making his own characters comment on the supposed meaninglessness and tedium of his plays. "This is becoming really insignificant," or, "It's awful. . . . Worse than the pantomime. . . .

The circus. . . . The music-hall. . . ." My favorite such comment, however, and perhaps Beckett's too, occurs in *Happy Days*. Winnie is recalling the remarks on her plight made by a Mr. Shower — or Cooker — who with his "fit mate" was the "last human kind — to stray this way":

> What's she doing? he says — What's the idea? he says — stuck up to her diddies in the bleeding ground — coarse fellow — What does it mean? he says — What's it meant to mean? — and so on — lot more stuff like that — usual drivel. . . .

This is the nearest equivalent one finds in Beckett to the prefaces of Racine quoted above, and its effect is the same: both playwrights are saying to their critics, "You blame me for doing what I have done, thinking it was the result of my tasteless stupidity. I assure you that on the contrary what I have done is exactly what I intended to do." Beckett has often stressed the strong unconscious impulses that partly control his writing; he has even spoken of being "in a trance" when he writes. Nevertheless, the quotation from *Happy Days* suggests that this play at least was the work of a supremely self-conscious artist, a latter-day Racine.

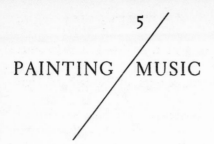

5

PAINTING / MUSIC

So far as I can judge, most of Beckett's knowledge of painting and sculpture has been acquired by tramping unwea-
riedly through museums and haunting exhibitions, rather
than from the written word. His published writings on
painting, scanty as they are, reveal a profound skepticism
about most art criticism, including his own:

> The best, that of a Fromentin, a Grohmann, a Mac-
> Greevy, a Sauerlandt, is so much Amiel. Hysterecto-
> mies done with a trowel. And how could it be otherwise?
> Can they even quote? When Grohmann demonstrates
> reminiscences of Mongol graphic art in Kandinsky,
> when MacGreevy so justly compares Yeats with Wat-
> teau, where do the rays of light fall? [*où vont les ray-
> ons?*] When Sauerlandt pronounces with finesse and —
> let's be just — parsimony upon the case of the great un-
> known painter that Ballmer is, where does that seed fall
> to earth? [*où cela retombe-t-il?*] *Das geht mich nicht
> an,** Ballmer used to say. . . .

* That's none of my business.

> Or else one produces general aesthetics, like Lessing.
> It's a charming game.
> Or else one produces anecdotes, like Vasari and Har-
> per's Magazine.
> Or else one makes *catalogues raisonnés*, like Smith.
> Or else one frankly gives oneself up to a disagreeable
> and confused chattering. That's the case here.[1]

Beckett thus damns with faint praise three of his contemporaries among art critics, while pouring contempt on
the great names of Vasari and Lessing. Fromentin is given
a suspended sentence, but the condemnation pronounced
on Beckett himself need not be taken too seriously: how
many of those who read the original French in *Cahiers
d'Art* in 1946 or later had the faintest idea what Yeats and
Ballmer had done, or even that the first was Irish, the second Swiss? In mentioning them at all, Beckett is backing
his own judgment against that of most contemporary art
critics. For that matter, the article in which his remarks
appeared was devoted to the praise of two other artists
equally unknown in Paris — though they had lived there off
and on for a number of years — the Dutchmen Geer and
Bram van Velde.

In an earlier critical article, his review of Thomas Mac-
Greevy's *Jack B. Yeats: An Appreciation and an Interpretation*, Beckett had written:

> There is at least this to be said for mind, that it can
> dispel mind. And at least this for art-criticism, that it
> can lift from the eyes, before *rigor vitae* sets in, some of
> the weight of congenital prejudice.[2]

Beckett's art criticism does attempt to lift this weight from
its reader's eyes and thus to benefit both the reader and,

ultimately, the artist whose work is under discussion. But, as we shall see, Beckett also "produces general aesthetics" in the course of writing about individual artists, especially Bram van Velde. Literary critics have suggested that *Three Dialogues* — in which Beckett attempts to define the aesthetic implicit in the work of Bram van Velde and to exalt it above that which he finds in the work of René-Pierre Tal-Coat, André Masson, or even the early Matisse — offers a better guide to Beckett's own aesthetic than to the painter's. I am not prepared to accept this view without modification. Those who draw conclusions about Beckett's aesthetic from his book on Proust have been seriously misled, I fear: only in the last section does he state his own views at all freely; the rest gives such a patient summary of the plot and method of *A la recherche du temps perdu* that students taking honors French at Trinity used to use it in preparing for degree examinations. Perhaps future art historians will applaud a similar patient fidelity in *Three Dialogues*.

Another important source of Beckett's knowledge of art besides gallery-going was his personal acquaintance with artists. Despite his parents' indifference to literature, some small awareness of painting must have reached him early from his father's side of the family. Beckett's Aunt Cissie, his father's sister, went to art school in Dublin and Paris; she afterwards married William ("Boss") Sinclair, a dealer in art and antiques in both Ireland and Germany, who naturally had artist friends in both countries. Beckett was in love for a time with his cousin Peggy Sinclair and visited her parents in Germany several times. One of Miss Beckett's close friends at art school was Estella ("Stella") Solomons (afterwards the wife of the poet "Seumas O'Sullivan," editor of *The Dublin Magazine*); another was Beatrice Elvery (afterwards Lady Glenavy): both these ladies were constant exhibitors at the Royal Hibernian Academy.

Beckett could hardly have escaped some knowledge of academic painting, at least, even before his month-long visit to Florence in the summer of 1927. When he went to Paris in October 1928, he had already been in Kassel with the Sinclairs the month before and had doubtless profited from William Sinclair's knowledge of contemporary German painting.[3] In Paris, MacGreevy, his predecessor as *lecteur d'anglais* at the Ecole Normale Supérieure, soon introduced him to James Joyce and thus, indirectly, to the entire Jolas circle. If Beckett did not then meet the artists who contributed to *Transition*, the magazine edited by Eugene Jolas, he must certainly have become aware of their work. Hans Arp and Man Ray were two of the most frequent contributors. It seems likely, however, that Beckett was too busy absorbing a whole new world of avant-garde literature, at the center of which stood Joyce's *Work in Progress*, to have the time or energy needed to assimilate avant-garde painting as well. At any rate, the only twentieth-century painter mentioned in *More Pricks Than Kicks* (1934) is the Irish academician Paul Henry. Rodin — or at least the Musée Rodin — is the only nineteenth-century artist named, but the Old Masters are well represented, especially the Italian Quattrocento: Botticelli, Perugino, Pisanello, Uccello, Benozzo (Gozzoli), Velasquez (twice), and Dürer. Leonardo's *Last Supper* is mentioned casually as "the Cena." Belacqua, the anti-hero of *More Pricks*, has been to Florence like his creator and recalls at least the outside of "the sinister Uffizi."

But it is in his native Dublin that he and Beckett have studied paintings most carefully. The "woman of the people" in "Ding-Dong" seems to Belacqua to have a remarkable face:

> Brimful of light and serene, serenissime, it bore no trace of suffering, and in this alone it might be said to be a notable face. Yet like tormented faces that he had seen, like the face in the National Gallery in Merrion Square by the Master of Tired Eyes, it seemed to have come a long way and [to] subtend an infinitely narrow angle of affliction, as eyes focus a star.

In "Love and Lethe" Beckett again turns to a specific painting in the same collection for help in describing a woman, Ruby Tough:

> Those who are in the least curious to know what she looked like at the time in which we have chosen to cull her we venture to refer to the Magdalene in the Perugino Pietà in the National Gallery of Dublin, always bearing in mind that the hair of our heroine is black and not ginger.

Beckett here speaks in his own person, as he does also in the footnote to the passage:

> This figure, owing to the glittering vitrine behind which the canvas cowers, can only be apprehended in sections. Patience, however, and a retentive memory have been known to elicit a total statement approximating to the intention of the painter.

"Patience . . . and a retentive memory," both of which Beckett possessed, are indispensable equipment for an art critic. We can also see from these quotations that he was at this time, like his future *persona* Murphy, "one of the elect, who require everything to remind them of something else."

In *Murphy* (1938), Beckett shows a knowledge of art that has been widened and deepened by his three-year stay in London (1933-36) and his art-hungry visits to Germany during 1936 and 1937, yet the novel contains significant references to only two contemporary artists, Braque and Barlach. The former is evoked by "a linoleum of exquisite design, a dim geometry of blue, grey and brown that delighted Murphy because it called Braque to his mind, and Celia because it delighted Murphy." The reference to the German sculptor occurs in a context which shows that Beckett must have been studying the history of ancient Greek and Hellenistic sculpture. Murphy is now a male nurse at the Magdalen Mental Mercyseat, where

> Murphy's first round had shown him what a mere phrase was Neary's "Sleep and Insomnia, the Phidias and Scopas of Fatigue." . . . Here those that slept and those that did not were quite palpably by the same hand, that of some rather later artist whose work could by no means have come down to us, say the Pergamene Barlach. And in his efforts to distinguish between the two groups Murphy was reminded of a wild waning winter afternoon in Toulon before the *hôtel de ville* and Puget's caryatids of Strength and Weariness, and the tattered sky blackening above his perplexity as to which was which.

Beckett's erudition here ranges over the history of sculpture from Periclean Athens to our own day. Phidias and his school of the fifth century B.C. are of course famous for the restraint and repose of their work, whereas that of Scopas and his school of the following century is notorious for violence and emotionalism. As for the Pergamene school of

Hellenistic sculpture, Beckett saw its greatest surviving monument, the altar of Zeus from Pergamon, during a visit to Berlin in December 1936 / January 1937. Murphy is imagining the existence of a Pergamene sculptor akin to Ernst Barlach, some of whose huddled figures — for example *Frierende Alte*, teakwood, 1937 — remind one irresistibly of characters in Beckett's later work. To fill the gap between Pergamon and modern Germany, Beckett throws in an idiosyncratic reference to Pierre Puget, the seventeenth-century French sculptor.

Since most of *Murphy* is set in or near London, it is appropriate that many of the specific works mentioned should be by English artists or else housed in London. We find references to the Harpy Tomb in the British Museum, to the bas-relief of W. H. Hudson's heroine Rima (by Jacob Epstein) in Hyde Park, to "the cast of the Physical Energy of G. F. Watts, O.M., R.A.," nearby, and to "Claude's Narcissus in Trafalgar Square" (i.e. in the National Gallery, Trafalgar Square). Murphy is at one point described as Blake's "conception of Bildad the Shuhite . . . come to life and . . . stalking about London in a green suit, seeking whom he might comfort." Perhaps the most erudite reference of all concerns the unlucky Hindu who "had been writing for many years . . . a monograph provisionally entitled: *The Pathetic Fallacy from Avercamp to Kampendonck*" and had "just . . . stumbled on the Norwich School for the first time" when he committed suicide. Beckett had become a connoisseur of Dutch and Flemish art during the years 1935-37, but one wonders whether he had done more than "stumble on" the landscapes of Cotman, Old Crome, and the rest of the Norwich School.

Other painters referred to in *Murphy* include Parmigianino, Tintoretto and Vermeer. After *Murphy*, however, Beckett's novels and plays virtually abandon all mention of specific painters and works of art. A notable exception is the comparison of Watt, with bloody face and hands, and thorns in his scalp, to "the Christ, believed by Bosch, then hanging in Trafalgar Square. . . ." Two other paintings are carefully described in *Watt*: the unattributed one in Erskine's room and another, mentioned in the "Addenda," which is ascribed to a non-existent painter named O'Connery. The only other exceptions I can think of are those unexpected references in *Malone Dies* to Kaspar David Friedrich, Tiepolo and Watteau to which I have drawn attention elsewhere.

Though Beckett rarely alluded to painters and sculptors in his creative writings after *Murphy*, his knowledge of twentieth-century art and artists really began after the virtual completion of that novel in 1936. Before that date, the only one on his personal list of modern masters that he knew well was Jack B. Yeats, whom he first met in late 1930, thanks to MacGreevy. On 22 December 1930 MacGreevy wrote to Yeats about Beckett's first visit: "I'm glad you liked him. He was completely staggered by the pictures and though he has met many people through me he dismissed them all in the letter with the remark 'and to think I owe meeting Jack Yeats *and* Joyce to you!' "[4] Beckett and Yeats soon became good friends, despite the thirty-five-year difference in their ages. Not until 1937 did Beckett again meet an artist of Yeats's stature, but in that year he met several of them, both in Germany and in France. Willi Grohmann, the art historian, whom he met in Dresden that year, opened many doors to him. On a second visit to Germany later that year, he met a number of artists of the current generation who had not yet made a name for themselves when Hitler came to power and were prevented from exhibiting thereafter because their art was supposed to be "decadent." Of these, the two who impressed Beckett most were Ballmer and Grimm;[5] the former, as we have already seen, became one of Beckett's unknown masters. It was in 1937 also, in Paris, that he met Geer and Bram van Velde; at first he was attracted more by the work of the former; not until after World War II did he decide that the latter was the greater artist. At this time also he met Marcel Duchamp, who had been famous since the days of Cubism and Dadaism: Duchamp professed to have given up painting altogether and to be more interested in chess, at which he was a master. Beckett played chess with him and seems to have shared his fascination with the end game.

Beckett published art criticism consists of the following six texts, which appeared during the years 1945-55:

A. "MacGreevy on Yeats" (written and published 1945);

B. "La Peinture des Van Velde ou le monde et le pantalon" (written January 1945, published 1946);

C. "Peintres de l'empêchement" (written and published 1948);

D. *Three Dialogues* (written and published 1949);

E. "Hommage à Jack B. Yeats" (written and published 1954);

F. "Henri Hayden, homme-peintre" (written January 1952, first published 1955).[6]

Perhaps the most important information to be gleaned
from these works is Beckett's own preference among twentieth-century artists: it may be a better guide to his aesthetic than all his enunciations of principle. We find him,
for instance, asserting of Jack B. Yeats in 1945 that "he is
with the great of our time, Kandinsky and Klee, Ballmer
and Bram van Velde, Rouault and Braque. . . ." (Note,
in passing, the tactical skill with which Beckett sandwiches
two virtually unknown painters whom he admires between
layers of the already well-known.) In a review of Denis
Devlin's poems published in 1938, he had already mentioned Braque and Klee with approval, linking their names
with that of the Norwegian Expressionist painter Edvard
Munch.[7] We have seen Beckett, in a quotation above from
the earliest of the Van Velde essays, implying approval of
Kandinsky as well as Ballmer and Yeats; later in the same
article he defends Dali's right to do what he does, without
expressing approval of the thing done; as for Picasso, Beckett
may admire him but insists that Homer often nods.

In "Peintres de l'empêchement," Beckett cites contemporary painters more freely, but he eliminates all the Surrealists from the discussion without naming any; he also
excludes "those estimable abstractors of quintessence, Mondrian, Lissitzky, Malevitsch, Moholy-Nagy." He is concerned rather to compare the Van Veldes with "inde-
pendents as diverse as Matisse, Bonnard, Villon, Braque,
Rouault, Kandinsky, to mention only them." Three new
names — Matisse, Bonnard, Villon — have here been added
to the canon. In *Three Dialogues*, however, Matisse ("of
the first period needless to say") and Bonnard, like Tal-
Coat and Masson, are mentioned as offering significant

approaches to art that must be rejected in favor of the approach adopted by Bram van Velde. Mondrian and Kandinsky are referred to also, with similar ambivalence. In "Hommage à Jack B. Yeats," the only painters named are Munch again and, for the first time, Ensor, as "sponsors" of Yeats, but they are promptly dismissed as "no great help." Henri Hayden has the distinction of being the only painter mentioned in the brief article consecrated to him. Although Beckett has not written about Alberto Giacometti, the Swiss sculptor, it seems to be generally agreed that he admires his work. Beckett also admires the graphics of the Israeli artist Avigdor Arikha, some of which have been to illustrate his fiction and so have attracted worldwide interest.

The publication of Beckett's *Still* in a limited edition of 160 copies at Milan in 1974, illustrated with three etchings by Stanley William Hayter, drew world-wide attention to one of Beckett's oldest friendships in the art world. Hayter, five years older than Beckett, founded the famous Atelier 17 in Paris in 1927. He illustrated volumes of poetry by Beckett's friends George Reavey and Brian Coffey during the 1930's and was a friend of MacGreevy's, so that Beckett may have met him during his first stay in Paris. Like Giacometti, for example, Hayter was powerfully influenced by Surrealism but later developed his own highly personal style. Although the final four-color versions of the *Still* etchings are disappointing — to me at least — it is impossible to set eyes on any of the three illustrations in their earlier black-and-white states without being powerfully reminded of Beckett. Anyone steeped in Beckett's work who came upon any or all of these graphics by chance would guess that they must relate to a Beckett text, even if the existence of *Still* were unknown to him. Hayter had once before, in 1957, used a Beckett text as the basis for a colored etching: *Poème* includes in its design an autograph copy of Beckett's quatrain "je voudrais que mon amour meure."[8]

What conclusions, quite independent of Beckett's theorizing, can we draw from a list of his favorites among the acknowledged masters of twentieth-century art? If we review the best-known work of Vassily Kandinsky, Paul Klee, Georges Rouault, Georges Braque, Munch, Pablo Picasso, Henri Matisse, Pierre Bonnard, Jacques Villon, James Ensor and Giacometti — leaving aside Piet Mondrian as an "abstractor of quintessence" — we find that these extraordinarily diverse artists have almost all at one time or another been described as Expressionists. On the one hand, with the exception of Kandinsky, they have never for long discarded the object from their works; on the other hand, with the possible exception of Matisse and Bonnard, they have never cared much for fidelity to the object as seen by the physical eye. Although respected in and for itself, the object nevertheless became for them an opportunity to reveal the inner world of the subject — i.e. the painter or sculptor. Even if Matisse and Bonnard did not seriously distort the form of the object, their use of color was subjective: what the French called *fauvisme* was never far from what the Germans called *Expressionismus*. The later work of Bram van Velde seems to me to resemble Abstract Expressionism.

It is easy to relate these painters' emphasis on subjectivity to the trend in Beckett's own work that culminated in *L'Innommable* (begun 1949). What must be stressed, however, is that Beckett never entirely abandoned the object in his work nor approved of painters who attempted to do so in theirs, not even the admired Kandinsky. The reference in *Three Dialogues* III to "the every man his own wife experiments of the spiritual Kandinsky" shows clearly, in my opinion, that Beckett did not — surely still does not — believe that the subject can become entirely its own object and continue to produce art. To attempt such a thing is the spiritual equivalent of masturbation. In fact, Beckett had already remarked in "Peintres de l'empêchement":

> It seems absurd to talk, as Kandinsky used to, of a painting freed from its object. What painting has freed itself from is the illusion that there exists more than one object of representation, perhaps even from the illusion that this unique object allows itself to be represented.[9]

This last quotation shows how close in spirit the Beckett of 1949 was to the Beckett of 1934, author of "Recent Irish Poetry." That early essay took as its main theme "the new thing that has happened, or the old thing that has happened again, namely the breakdown of the object. . . ." Beckett admitted that this could be "amended to breakdown of the subject."

> It comes to the same thing — rupture of the lines of communication.
> The artist who is aware of this may state the space that intervenes between him and the world of objects. . . . A picture by Mr. Jack Yeats, Mr. Eliot's "Waste Land," are notable statements of this kind. Or he may celebrate the cold comforts of apperception. He may even record his findings, if he is a man of great personal courage.[10]

This is, I think, Beckett's first published tribute to Jack
Yeats, who finds himself in exalted company. *The Waste
Land* may well have represented Beckett's poetic ideal at
that time. The essay judges contemporary Irish poets according to their awareness of the "rupture," the "bankrupt
relationship," between subject and object. One wonders
what or who it was that first made Beckett himself aware
of that rupture. Was it Werner Heisenberg's Uncertainty
Principle, Einstein's Relativity Theory, the phenomenology
of Husserl, Berkeley's *esse est percipi* ("to be is to be perceived"), or simply paintings by precisely those contemporary artists of whom we have been speaking?

Lawrence E. Harvey regards "La Peinture des Van Velde"
as the "most important of Beckett's essays on the Van
Velde brothers."[11] Much as I enjoy the ironic wit and
humor of this essay, I cannot quite agree with Harvey about
its importance, if only because it never mentions the breakdown of the object nor the bankruptcy of the subject-object
relationship. Although "Peintres de l'empêchement," a
shorter essay, does duplicate some of the points made by
its predecessor, it introduces the notion of *le deuil de l'objet*
("mourning for the object"), whereas the earlier essay
speaks of the *objectivité prodigieuse* of Abraham (Bram)
van Velde. Perhaps, however, this objectivity is not incom-
patible with the breakdown of the object, for Beckett makes
clear that it has nothing to do with the objectivity of the
conventional realist. The painting of the elder Van Velde,
he suggests, is "primarily a painting of the thing in a state
of suspense," of suspended animation, almost.

> It is the thing alone, isolated by the need to see it, by
> the need to see. The thing immobile in the void, there

> at last is the thing visible, the pure object. I don't see
> that there is any other.
>
> The brain-pan has the monopoly of this article.
>
> It is there that time sometimes comes to rest, like the
> wheel of the electric meter when the last bulb goes out.
>
> It is there, in the dark, that one at last begins to see.
> In the dark that no longer fears any dawn. In the dark
> that is dawn and midday and evening and night of an
> empty sky and an unmoving earth. In the dark* that
> enlightens the spirit.[12]

(Note the paradox that "the pure object" exists only within
the brain-pan and is thus purely subjective.) Whether or
not this is a true description of the vision of Bram van
Velde, it certainly provides the perfect metaphor for Beckett's own achievement in *L'Innommable*.

Where Bram van Velde turns inward, Gerardus (Geer)
van Velde turns outward, according to Beckett. His work is
centrifugal rather than centripetal. Instead of stillness, there
is movement:

> Here all moves, swims, flees, returns, unmakes itself.
> All ceases, unceasingly. One would think it was the in-
> surrection of the molecules, the interior of a stone one-
> thousandth of a second before it disintegrates.[13]

At the risk of being ridiculous, Beckett decides to put the
difference between the brothers in the crudest terms, saying that Bram "paints extension," whereas Geer "paints
succession," or, as Beckett later puts it, concerns himself
"less with an object than with a process [*processus*]." Their
respective bodies of work "seem to refute each other, but in
fact meet at the heart of the dilemma, that indeed of the

---

* Compare what Krapp says about "the dark" (see above, p. 6).

plastic arts in general: How to represent change?" Both the
Van Veldes have given up attempting this impossible task;
instead, Bram has chosen to represent "the thing that suffers, the thing that is changed," while his brother has taken
for his share "the thing that inflicts, the thing that causes
change." Beckett concludes his essay by returning to a paradox he had stated earlier: the brothers Van Velde "are at
bottom uninterested in painting; what interests them is
the human condition." In the post-war mood of contrition,
when everybody is mouthing platitudes about "the human"
and about collective effort, he wonders, "What will become
of . . . this solitary painting . . . whose least fragment
contains more true humanity than all their processions towards a happiness like that of a sacrificial sheep. I suppose
it will be pelted with stones."

In "Peintres de l'empêchement," Beckett discusses the
work of the Van Velde brothers less for its own sake than
as a pretext for generalizing about contemporary art as a
whole. The argument proper begins with the statement that
"the history of painting is the history of its relationship with
its object. . . ." This relationship is naturally first explored
in terms of breadth, then in terms of depth or penetration:
as painting becomes conscious of its limitations, it explores
the outer confines of those limitations and then turns towards exploration in depth, towards *la chose que cache la
chose* ("the thing hidden behind the thing").

> The object of representation always resists representa-
> tion, either because of its accidents or because of its
> substance. . . .
> The first attack mounted against the object seized, in-
> dependently of its qualities, in its indifference, its iner-

tia, its latency — *there's* a definition of modern painting no more ridiculous than any other.[14]

It is this definition that eliminates the Surrealists, who are only interested "in questions of repertory" — meaning, I imagine, that most Surrealists represent the object in a fairly academic way: what interests them is odd selections and collocations of objects. This definition also eliminates the "abstractors of quintessence." Those that the definition covers, however diverse they may be, are engaged in a common pursuit:

> Rouault's Christs, the most Chinese still-life by Matisse, a conglomerate by the Kandinsky of 1943 or 1944, are products of the same effort — to express how a clown, an apple and a square of red are all one — and of the same disarray, facing the resistance put up by this uniqueness against being expressed. For they are only one in this respect, that they are things, the thing, thingness.[15]

The hindrances to expression are of two kinds. One type of artist will say:

> I can't see the object, in order to represent it, because it is what it is. The other: I can't see the object, to represent it, because I am what I am.
>
> There have always been these two kinds of artist, these two kinds of hindrance, the object-hindrance and the eye-hindrance. People took account of these hindrances. An accommodation was reached. They did not form part of the representation, or scarcely so. Here [in the work of the Van Veldes] they do form part. The greater part, one might say. What hinders from painting is painted [*Est peint ce qui empêche de peindre*].
>
> Geer van Velde is an artist of the first kind (in my stumbling opinion), Bram van Velde of the second.

> Their painting is an analysis of a state of privation,
> borrowing on the part of the one the terms of the with-
> out, light and the void, on the part of the other those
> of the within, darkness, the plenum, phosphorescence.

This contrast is developed for two more paragraphs and
ends with an unforgettable image of Bram's work: "cellule
peinte sur la pierre de la cellule, art d'incarcération" ("cell
painted on the stone wall of a cell, an art of incarceration").
The article concludes with a magisterial summation, in
which the Van Veldes are presented as the true heirs of the
best in modern painting, and also as pioneers leading the
way to the painting of the future:

> The painting of the Van Veldes, free of all concern
> with criticism, emerges from a painting of criticism and
> refusal, refusal to accept the old subject-object relation-
> ship as a given.

There are now three roads that painting can choose, of
which the third is

> the road forward of a . . . painting of acceptance, fore-
> seeing, in the absence of a relationship and the absence
> of an object, the new relationship and the new object, a
> road already dividing into two branches in the respective
> labors of Bram and Greer van Velde.

The *Three Dialogues* have drawn such wide attention
since their publication in book form that they may seem to
need no lengthy commentary or quotation here. What
could be more familiar to Beckett addicts than this exchange, from the first dialogue?

> D. [Georges Duthuit] — And preferring what?
> B. [Beckett] — The expression that there is nothing to

express, nothing with which to express, nothing from which to express, no power to express, no desire to express, together with the obligation to express.

B.'s preference is for the art of Bram van Velde, as we discover in the third dialogue, but inevitably the critics apply this description to Beckett's own art as well. In doing so, they encourage us to ignore the earlier passages of the dialogue, where Beckett strives to do justice to the art of René-Pierre Tal-Coat. He sees in it "a thrusting towards a more adequate expression of natural experience. . . ." When Duthuit objects, "But that which this painter discovers, orders, transmits, is not in nature," Beckett insists: "By nature I mean here . . . a composite of perceiver and perceived, not a datum, an experience. All I wish to suggest is that the tendency and accomplishment of this painting are fundamentally those of previous painting. . . ." Beckett does not object to the Italian painters because "they surveyed the world with the eyes of building contractors" but because "they never stirred from the field of the possible, however much they may have enlarged it. The only thing disturbed by the revolutionaries Matisse and Tal Coat is a certain order on the plane of the feasible." Admitting his illogicality, Beckett wants an art that turns from the feasible "in disgust." As Duthuit is made to say, "But that is a violently extreme and personal point of view, of no help to us in the matter of Tal Coat." Nevertheless, Beckett's previous remarks have set the revolutionary claims of Matisse and Tal-Coat — not to mention the entire history of Italian painting — in a new light. They are a contribution to the history of art, or at any rate of art criticism, as well as to the history of the growth of a poet's mind.

The second dialogue deals with André Masson, who holds less interest for Beckett than Tal-Coat. Duthuit does most of the talking, quoting frequently from Masson's own discussions of his work; Beckett at intervals registers polite dissent and ends by saying, "So forgive me if I relapse, as when we spoke of the so different Tal Coat, into my dream of an art unresentful of its insuperable indigence and too proud for the farce of giving and receiving." Duthuit answers him once more, ending with a rhetorical question:

> Are we really to deplore the painting that is a rallying, among the things of time that pass and hurry us away, towards a time that endures and gives increase?
> B. — (Exit weeping.)

Each of the first two dialogues begins with a brief statement from Beckett, presumably because the *casus belli* has been chosen by his adversary. At the beginning of the third dialogue, however, since the subject, Bram van Velde, is of his own choosing, Beckett says punctiliously, "Frenchman, fire first." In the event, however, Duthuit allows him to state his position clearly and then pushes him to its logical limit:

> D. — One moment. Are you suggesting that the painting of van Velde is inexpressive?
> B. — (a fortnight later) Yes.
> D. — You realise the absurdity of what you advance?
> B. — I hope I do.
> D. — What you say amounts to this: the form of expression known as painting . . . has had to wait for van Velde to be rid of the misapprehension under which it has laboured so long and so bravely, namely, that its function was to express, by means of paint.
> B. — Others have felt that art is not necessarily expression.

But the numerous attempts made to make painting independent of its occasion have only succeeded in en-
larging its repertory. I suggest that van Velde is the first
whose painting is bereft, rid if you prefer, of occasion
in every shape and form, ideal as well as material, and
the first whose hands have not been tied by the certi-
tude that expression is an impossible act.

Beckett — who now is using "occasion," apparently as a
less question-begging term, in place of "object" — refuses
to concede that the very absence of occasion is itself an
occasion. Duthuit demands that he should "make some
kind of connected statement and then go away." Beckett,
by now a master of serio-comic dialogue, with the manuscript of *En attendant Godot* in his drawer, asks, "Would
it not be enough if I simply went away?" Duthuit, however,
insists that he finish what he has begun, admonishing Beckett in words that the critics have refused, perhaps rightly, to
take to heart: "Try and bear in mind that the subject under
discussion is not yourself, nor the Sufist Al-Haqq, but a particular Dutchman by name van Velde, hitherto erroneously
referred to as an *artiste peintre*."

It need surprise nobody that Beckett's connected statement is chiefly concerned with "the relation between the
artist and his occasion" — our old friend the subject-object
relationship, whose breakdown Beckett had recognized at
least fifteen years earlier. "The history of painting, here we
go again, is the history of its attempts to escape from this
sense of failure" provoked by the instability of the relation;
it inspires "a kind of Pythagorean terror, as though the irrationality of pi were an offence against the deity, not to mention his creature." Subject and object, then, are incom-

mensurable, just as the radius and circumference of a circle (or the side and diagonal of a square, another favorite Beckett example) are incommensurable, or as God and man are.

> My case, since I am in the dock, is that van Velde is . . . the first to submit wholly to the incoercible absence of relation, . . . the first to admit that to be an artist is to fail, as no other dare fail, that failure is his world. . . .

Beckett once again refuses

> to make of this submission, . . . this fidelity to failure, a new occasion, a new term of relation, and of the act which, unable to act, obliged to act, he makes, an expressive act. . . . For what is this coloured plane, that was not there before. I don't know what it is, having never seen anything like it before. It seems to have nothing to do with art, in any case, if my memories are correct.

He is about to go when Duthuit reminds him that he had promised to say something more:

> B. — (Remembering, warmly) Yes, yes, I am mistaken, I am mistaken.[16]

Having loaded Bram van Velde with all the sins and errors of European art and driven him out into the wilderness to make expiation, Beckett rescues him at the last moment by a retraction, but only on the condition, we feel, that he himself shall become the scapegoat.

Having developed his aesthetic theory to its natural limit in *Three Dialogues*, Beckett retired from controversy. His two other articles on painting are brief, elegant tributes to individual artists. The first to be written, that on Henri

Hayden, refers once again to what it calls "the subject-object crisis." Hayden's method of coping with this crisis is presented as unique, yet similar enough to Beckett's own to arouse his "fraternal affection." The tribute begins by quoting Gautama Buddha as saying "that one is mistaken in affirming that the I exists, but in affirming that it does not exist one is equally mistaken." Beckett finds an echo of this "crazy wisdom" in Hayden's canvases "and, very quietly, of its corollary, to wit that the same is true of the rest" (*le reste*, presumably equivalent to "the not-I").

> Bare presence of him who makes, bare presence of what is made. Impersonal work, unreal work. It is a very curious thing, this double effacement. And very haughty in its untopicality. The subject-object crisis is not at the end of its best days. But it is separately and to the benefit of one or the other that we are used to seeing this clown and his Auguste collapse. Whereas here, confounded in a shared unsubstantiality, they abdicate in concert.[17]

In an evocative passage, Beckett gives his impression of Hayden's landscapes and still-lifes, noting "how fragile is their touching assurance of familiar forms and all the equivocation of these trees that give up as soon as they have started, of these fruits that seem the victims of miscasting" ("de ces arbres qui abandonnent assitôt partis, de ces fruits qu'on dirait victimes d'une erreur de distribution"). The delicacy and indeterminacy of the description rival those of the work described. Beckett ends by regretting that he "had not been sufficiently astonished" at the existence of a "calmly hopeless" painter who not merely does not run away from the mirages, the intermittences and the illusory intercommunication of a self such as it is and an unpossessable Nature but endures them and coaxes from them a body of work scaled to the famishing measure of Man. . . .

This may seem faint enough praise for the painter who had somewhat cheered his exile in Roussillon, 1942-44, but it was praise of a sort that would have made Beckett himself very happy when the article was written in January 1952.

Beckett's last public tribute to Jack Yeats is indeed an act of homage: he must have realized that the painter, nearly eighty-three, could not survive much longer. In fact, Yeats gave up painting the next year and died in 1957. It was no time to use the old master as a pretext for polemic, whether against Ireland or against international art criticism. Instead, Beckett chose to make a positive dogmatic statement stressing Yeats's inner vision, his uniqueness, his technical mastery, and then — "S'incliner simplement, émerveillé." The text is so short and yet so cryptic that I have thought it worth while to quote it in full in my own translation, which is also, of course, an interpretation:

> The incomparable thing about this great solitary body of work is its insistence on sending us back to the most secret recess of the spirit that animates it and on not allowing itself to be illumined by any other light.
> Hence this unexampled strangeness, which the customary references to heritage, national or otherwise, leave undiminished. What could have less to do with Fairyland than this marvelous workmanship, prompted as it were by the thing to be done and by its own urgency? As for the sponsors that have finally been un-

earthed for him, Ensor and Munch leading the parade, the least one can say about them is that they are no great help to us.

The artist who stakes his whole being comes from nowhere. And he has no brothers.

Should one expatiate, then? On these fiercely immediate images that leave no place or time for comforting feats of skill. On this violence of need that unleashes the images and sends them flying beyond their horizons. On this vast inner reality where phantoms dead and alive, Nature and Void, all that never ends and all that will never be, unite in a single testimony, delivered once for all.

Finally, on this supreme mastery that submits to the unmasterable, and trembles.

No.

Simply bow down, in wonderment.

The most poignant paragraph here, and the most autobiographical, perhaps, is the third: "L'artiste qui joue son être est de nulle part. Et il n'a pas de frères." Like so much that seems simple in this text, it is full of ambiguity. The great artist comes from nowhere, as if he sprang from the head of Zeus; but Beckett is also insisting, as he did in "MacGreevy on Yeats," that "the national aspects of Mr. Yeats's genius . . . have been over-stated, and for motives not always remarkable for their aesthetic purity." I have taken the liberty of expanding "Quoi de moins féerique . . . ?" into "What could have less to do with Fairyland . . . ?" because I think Beckett means specifically to dissociate Yeats from the Celtic twilight. In saying that the great artist has no brothers, Beckett is not merely stressing freedom from family ties or from fraternal debts to artists in the same tradition (Ensor, Munch); he is reminding us that Jack Yeats had a brother who was widely considered a very great poet, though perhaps not by Beckett. Also, consciously or unconsciously, Beckett is claiming on his own behalf freedom from all indebtedness, whether artistic, national, or familial. Jack B. Yeats, Bram van Velde, and the other solitary painters Beckett has admired have all confirmed the example of Joyce in encouraging him to become just such another solitary explorer of interior space.

When we turn from painting to music, the effect is one of almost total antithesis. True, Beckett is an amateur in both arts, but in painting he is a passive one — "amateur bien sage, tel que les peintres le rêvent, qui arrive les bras ballants et les bras ballants s'en va, la tête lourde de ce qu'il a cru entrevoir"*[18] — whereas in music he is active, an amateur performer on the piano and, at one time, on the flute. In painting, as we have seen, his taste was at first for traditional if not conventional work but moved fairly quickly in the direction of the contemporary and the avant-garde; in music, however, his taste seems to have remained essentially traditional. Again, whereas in his early works — criticism, poetry, fiction — he likes to make a parade of his hard-won knowledge of the fine arts, his references to music are generally much less esoteric and pretentious. Paintings and sculptures are always called on to provide a specific comparison, whereas music from the beginning has a more general symbolic value; Eugene Webb suggests also that some of the later works are consciously modeled on musical forms.[19] Finally, whereas décor is at a minimum in all the

* A well-behaved amateur, such as painters dream of, who arrives with arms dangling and goes off again, arms dangling, his head heavy with what he believes he has caught a glimpse of.

stage plays, all the radio plays — and also *Act Without Words I* and *Happy Days* — owe at least part of their impact to music: indeed, music itself is a "character" in *Words and Music* and *Cascando*, both of which could be described as libretti rather than radio dramas.

It seems to have been taken for granted in the Beckett family that music was a more essential part of culture than either literature or the fine arts: unlike similar middle-class families in Ireland and England, they expected boys as well as girls to study the piano. Not only did Samuel and his elder brother Frank take lessons but so did their first cousins John and Peter Beckett, and their first cousin on the mother's side, Jack Roe. At Portora, Frank and Sam continued to study the piano. A contemporary of Sam's there commented on how unusual it was for boys in their last two years to take music lessons, as Sam did.[20] Music was not a part of the regular curriculum, except for very young boys who sang in the choir. Music lessons, as well as practice time, had to be scheduled outside regular school hours and paid for as an "extra," over and above the regular tuition fees. I don't know whether Beckett ever took formal lessons in musical theory, either at Portora or earlier, but he has picked up enough of the subject to make the following rather technical allusions in *Murphy:*

> 1. [Murphy's vagitus] had not been the proper A of international concert pitch, with 435 double vibrations per second, but the double flat of this. How he winced, the honest obstetrician, a devout member of the old Dublin Orchestral Society, and an amateur flautist of some merit.

2. A kiss from Wylie was like a breve tied, in a long slow amorous phrase, over bars' times its equivalent in demi-semiquavers.

3. [Murphy] kissed her, in Lydian mode, and went to the door.

4. The decaying Haydn, invited to give his opinion of cohabitation, replied: "Parallel thirds." But the partition of Miss Counihan and Wylie had more concrete grounds.

Furthermore, in the "Addenda" to *Watt*, the description of the second picture in Erskine's room includes the following: "With his right hand he sustains a chord which Watt has no difficulty in identifying as that of C major in its second inversion. . . ." Although these passages are all impenetrable to someone who knows nothing of musical terminology, they are hardly of the same order of difficulty as, say, the reference to "the Pergamene Barlach" in *Murphy*.

As for Beckett's taste in music, at Portora he was known as a lover of Gilbert and Sullivan, allegedly able to play and sing whole operettas from memory. In early manhood he played Chopin and Schubert badly but with energy and on one occasion *hummed* entire Beethoven sonatas. In *More Pricks than Kicks* we find references both to composers — Chopin, Auber, John Field — and to specific works: "Scarlatti's Capriccio," "Ravel's Pavane [for a Dead Infanta]," Schubert's song "An die Musik," Mozart's *Don Giovanni*, and "any Mozart [piano] sonata whatsoever . . . in Augener's edition." On a less exalted plane, we read of "the totem chorus . . . in Rose Marie," perhaps the most lowbrow musical reference to be found anywhere in Beckett's work. In *Murphy*, the only composer named besides Haydn is Samuel Coleridge-Taylor.

It is in the plays, however, that Beckett can fully use the power of music to stir our emotions. Surely nobody who has seen *Happy Days* can forget the poignancy of both the tune (as played by a music-box) and the words (as sung by Winnie) of the too-familiar *Merry Widow* waltz: any music less hackneyed and less sweet would have thwarted the full tragicomic impact of the final moments. A more purely tragic use is made of Schubert's *Death and the Maiden* at the beginning and end of the radio play *All That Fall*, in which Mrs. Rooney's dead or perhaps unborn daughter is evoked; a little child also is run over by Mr. Rooney's train. *Embers*, which owes so much of its effect to the constant beat of sea on shingle, allows little scope for music, but we do hear Henry's child, Addie, at her music lesson, struggling with "Chopin's 5th Waltz in A Flat Major"; the comic pathos of the unwilling or untalented music student is underlined by Henry's sardonic remark: "It was not enough to drag her into the world, now she must play the piano."

This chapter has attempted to assess, almost entirely on the basis of internal evidence drawn from his own writings, the dimensions of Beckett's knowledge of the fine arts and music. It would be impossible, I believe, to deny that this knowledge is extensive — and to some degree intensive — in both areas. As we have seen, however, it was acquired in radically different ways: Beckett learned about music as a schoolboy and as a performer concerned with practical problems rather than with theory; because of this initiation, probably, he wrote no music criticism. On the other hand, he gained his knowledge of painting and sculpture mainly as an adult who had never practiced either art himself except for childhood dabblings in water-color and who, in spite of his frequent denials, was deeply interested in problems of aesthetic theory, discussed in his critical articles. As a direct consequence of the difference between his artistic and his musical educations, apparently, Beckett developed a wide and deep knowledge of contemporary painting and sculpture, while showing virtually no interest in contemporary music except when, late in his life, musicians asked for his collaboration.

In the next chapter I shall try to answer the question: How much does Beckett's literary style appeal to the eye and how much to the ear? Let me only say now that, *a priori*, one might assume that Beckett's visual awareness, developed so cerebrally and almost painfully, could never match his aural awareness, developed so early and, relatively speaking, unconsciously. But the matter may not turn out to be quite so simple as it appears.

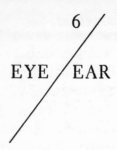

6

EYE / EAR

The most curious aspect of Beckett's published art criticism is his failure to describe a single individual work of art. He sometimes produces, as we have seen, memorable verbal formulations of the general effect of an artist's work, but what Mr. Kelly in *Murphy* called "demented particulars" are not to be found. When we turn to the much wider terrain of Beckett's creative work with this fact in mind, we realize that, apart from the two imaginary paintings described in *Watt*, few and fragmentary specifics are to be found there either. The most precise description that I can recall occurs in *Murphy*; it is brief enough and concerns only a detail of the total work: "He saw the clenched fists and rigid upturned face of the Child in a Giovanni Bellini Circumcision, waiting to feel the knife." Much more typical of Beckett's treatment of specific pictures in his early work is his comparison of the heroine of "Love and Lethe" to "the Magdalene in the Perugino Pietà in the National Gallery of Dublin." Far from describing either Ruby Tough or the Magdalene, he assumes, no doubt tongue-in-cheek, the reader's hard-won knowledge of an ill-framed, ill-lighted painting,* and asks him to accept this as a description of Ruby, "always bearing in mind that the hair of our heroine is black not ginger." This whole passage is, on one level, a complex comic device by which the self-conscious narrator abandons all pretense of realistic narrative while at the same time laying claim to an objective accuracy unsurpassed in literature — always provided that the reader is familiar with the painting. Despite the over-all comic tone of *Watt*, a similar device may be used in that novel with more serious intent:

> [Watt's] face was bloody, his hands also, and thorns were in his scalp. (His resemblance, at that moment, to the Christ believed by Bosch, then hanging in Trafalgar Square, was so striking, that I remarked it.)

Here we are in fact given some description of Watt before the reference to the painting; the chief purpose of the latter may therefore be to suggest that Watt is Christ-like, as are so many of the clowns portrayed by Beckett and by Rouault. This passage, however, is the last of its kind that I can recall in Beckett's work. There are a couple of surprising references to art and artists in *Malone Dies*, but they do not involve specific details of paintings. At one point Malone remarks:

> It is such a night as Kaspar David Friedrich loved, tempestuous and bright. That name comes back to me, those names. The clouds scud, tattered by the wind, across a limpid ground.

* See above, p. 92.

Elsewhere he speaks of

> this window that sometimes looks as if it were painted
> on the wall, like Tiepolo's ceiling at Würzburg, what a
> tourist I must have been, I even remember the diaeresis
> [*Umlaut*], if it is one.

I can see at least two reasons for the abandonment of
such references to specific paintings. The more immediately
obvious is that they are of course only possible when the
protagonist and / or the narrator is self-consciously cul-
tured, a "highbrow," as he is in *More Pricks Than Kicks*,
Murphy, and *Watt*. The narrator of *Mercier et Camier*
(written in 1946) has much in common with his predecessors, expressing self-conscious judgments on his own style in
phrases like "Que cela pue l'artifice" ("What stink of artifice"). But the recondite allusions in this book have nothing to do with the fine arts or music. Though occasionally
historical or scientific, they are chiefly literary — Homer,
Vauvenargues, Dante (twice) — or biblical. After 1946, the
Beckett narrator (Moran in *Molloy* always excepted) either
does not know such things or has forgotten them so completely that if they turn up in his narrative, they surprise
him at least as much as the reader: for example, Malone's
reference to Tiepolo and Würzburg.

The other reason for not making such allusions is that
they are useless to the reader if he is not familiar with the
painting in question: he must either go to Dublin and visit
the National Gallery or remain forever ignorant of the features of Ruby Tough. Beckett may even succeed in either
angering or humiliating such an uninformed reader. Indeed,
this may have been his secret intention. By the time he be-

gan to write *Molloy*, however, as he told me in 1973, Beckett had become convinced that he knew nothing: it was in
this spirit that the trilogy was written, and although the old
intellectual arrogance flashed out from time to time in his
art criticism, as we have seen, it never again intruded into
his creative work to quite the same degree.

It is possible to argue that if the reader *did* know the
work of art referred to, he would obtain from Beckett's narrative an impression unique in its accuracy. But in that
case, why not illustrate one's novels and short stories with
reproductions from the Old Masters? It was not until he
had written some plays that Beckett realized a self-evident
fact: drama can borrow from the existing treasury of music
far more effectively than narrative fiction can borrow from
that of the fine arts. It was his first radio play, *All That Fall*,
that reminded Beckett of the possibilities of music; later, in
Happy Days, he made similar use of music in a play for the
stage. As we shall see, he did not fully release the power
latent in music until he collaborated with living composers
in the radio plays *Cascando* and *Words and Music*.

When we re-read that description of a Bellini "Circumcision," with "the clenched fists and rigid upturned face of
the Child . . . waiting to feel the knife," we become aware
that Beckett has not only looked at the painting with great
attention and interpreted it with sensitivity, he has also expressed what he has seen in words of extreme vividness. The
visual qualities in Beckett's writing have not, I think, been
done justice by his critics. Many of them first became aware
of him through *Waiting for Godot*, in which whole passages take on the rhythm of verse. Others encountered him
first in the trilogy, where visual effects often seem minimal

("no light / But rather darkness visible"), especially in *The Unnamable,* whose reader is above all conscious of the endless stream of the spoken word — now a torrent, now a trickle, but always suggestive of a water imagery that is more aural than visual.

Those who, like myself, first became aware of Beckett as the author of *Murphy* have a more balanced impression. Look, for instance, at the famous conclusion of Chapter 12, where Cooper disposes of Murphy's ashes:

> He was turning into the station, without having met any considerable receptacle for refuse, when a burst of music made him halt and turn. It was the pub across the way, opening for the evening session. The lights sprang up in the saloon, the doors burst open, the radio struck up. He crossed the street and stood on the threshold. The floor was palest ochre, the pin-tables shone like silver, the quoits board had a net, the stools the high rungs that he loved, the whiskey was in glass tanks, a slow cascando of pellucid yellows. . . .
>
> Some hours later Cooper took the packet of ash from his pocket, where earlier in the evening he had put it for greater security, and threw it angrily at a man who had given him great offence. It bounced, burst, off the wall on to the floor, where at once it became the object of much dribbling, passing, trapping, shooting, punching, heading and even some recognition from the gentleman's code. By closing time the body, mind and soul of Murphy were freely distributed over the floor of the saloon; and before another dayspring greyened the earth had been swept away with the sand, the beer, the butts, the glass, the matches, the spits, the vomit.

It may seem extravagant to submit a piece of such low comedy to close analysis, but careful writing deserves careful reading. There can be no doubt about the care with which the passage was written. Look, for instance, at the verbs in the third sentence — "sprang," "burst," "struck." Each is a monosyllabic Anglo-Saxon "strong" verb, and each by its brevity and stress on intense action emphasizes the abruptness with which temptation seized the alcoholic Cooper. We see and hear simultaneously: probably no one had ever before written that "the radio struck up" — it was always the band that did so — but it seems perfectly appropriate here. After a fairly neutral sentence that brings Cooper to the threshold, we have a sentence full of visual imagery that makes us see a very ordinary saloon bar through his eyes — or, rather, his single eye — as a palace of art. Yet this sentence, at first seemingly directed solely at the eye, ends with a feast for the ear in the long vowels and hesitating rhythm of "a slow cascando of pellucid yellows." Even the hiatus between the two successive "o" sounds adds to the charm of the phrase. Still, the main strength of the first paragraph lies in its visual appeal, whereas that of the second seems at first completely aural. The sequence of six dissyllabic verbal nouns — "dribbling, passing," etc. — and the later series of monosyllables are chiefly responsible for this impression; yet one cannot afford to ignore the visual precision of "It bounced, burst, off the wall on to the floor. . . ." The words "bounced, burst" have an onomatopoetic effect as well, of course, besides their obvious alliteration. The final list of rejectamenta has a cruel visual accuracy, but in the end it is the rhythm that once again predominates. Note particularly the dying fall achieved by ending with an unstressed syllable. To have concluded with "the vomit, the spits" would have destroyed the whole cadence.

The art of this little exercise in black humor surprises us
by its delicacy and precision, but in the next and final chapter, where Beckett is clearly reaching out for pathos, the
blending of aural and visual stimuli puts the reader completely at his mercy: even if he recognizes Beckett's conscious artifice, he is compelled to surrender. The chapter
begins rather cheerfully, with a strong emphasis on the
visual:

> Late afternoon, Saturday, October the 26th. A mild
> clear, sunless day, sudden gentle eddies of rotting leaves,
> branches still against the still sky, from a chimney a pine
> of smoke.

Nevertheless, a detail like the repetition of "still" or the
frequent use of "l" sounds will remind us that the ear is not
being wholly neglected. By the end of the chapter, when
Mr. Kelly has flown his kite out of sight and then lost it and
when we have realized that his niece, Celia, having herself
lost Murphy, has returned to the oldest profession, Beckett
is making almost intolerable demands upon eye and ear —
the whole punctuated by the park rangers' "wail" of *All
out.*

> *All out. All out.*
> Mr. Kelly *tottered* to his feet, *tossed* up his arms high
> and wide and quavered away down the path that led to
> the water, a ghastly, lamentable figure. The slicker
> *trailed* along the ground, the skull *gushed* from under
> the cap like a dome from under its lantern, the ravaged
> face was a cramp of bones, throttled sounds jostled in
> his throat.
> Celia caught him on the margin of the pond. The
> end of the line *skimmed* the water, *jerked* upward in a
> wild whirl, *vanished* joyfully in the dusk. Mr. Kelly went

limp in her arms. Someone fetched the chair and
helped to get him aboard. Celia *toiled* along the narrow
path into the teeth of the wind, then faced north up
the wide hill. There was no shorter way home. The
yellow hair *fell* across her face. The yachting cap *clung*
like a clam to the skull. The levers were the tired heart.
She closed her eyes.
   All out.

Tiny Mr. Kelly, with his huge head and his yachting cap, is
seen to be pathetic as well as grotesque, pitiable as well as
ridiculous, in his grief over the lost kite, whose string leaps
and whirls before our eyes like a live thing. (Note the visual
impact of the verbs I have italicized.) Until one reads the
passage aloud, the visual may seem dominant — especially
if one can see the levers of the self-propelling invalid chair
as they beat the air slowly and vainly in the rhythm of "the
tired heart." Read aloud, however, the progressively shorter
and shorter sentences describing Celia's struggle up the hill
suggest the diminishing speed of her progress and her growing exhaustion. And nothing could be more final than that
last spondaic *All out*.
   It would be futile to look for passages of comparable
power in *Watt*, a transitional work pointing towards the
subjectivity of the fiction in French that succeeded it.
Though the dialogue in *Watt* and *Mercier et Camier* seems
lively and full of surface realism, narrative and description
are losing objectivity, becoming internalized. The beginning of a shorter work of the same period, *L'Expulsé* (*The
Expelled*), offers a comic example of internalized description and its pitfalls. The narrator doubtless intends to describe for us the steps down which he falls when he is ex-

pelled from his boyhood home; this is the result of his attempt:

> There were not many steps. I had counted them a thousand times, both going up and coming down, but the figure has gone from my mind. I have never known whether you should say one with your foot on the sidewalk, two with the following foot on the first step, and so on, or whether the sidewalk shouldn't count. At the top of the steps I fell foul of the same dilemma. In the other direction, I mean from top to bottom, it was the same, the word is not too strong. I did not know where to begin nor where to end, that's the truth of the matter. I arrived therefore at three totally different figures, without ever knowing which of them was right. And when I say that the figure has gone from my mind, I mean that none of the three figures is with me any more, in my mind. It is true that if I were to find, in my mind, where it is certainly to be found, one of these figures, I would find it and it alone, without being able to deduce from it the other two. And even were I to recover two, I would not know the third. No, I would have to find all three, in my mind, in order to know all three. . . .
>
> After all it is not the number of steps that matters. The important thing to remember is that there were not many, and that I have remembered. Even for the child there were not many, compared to other steps he knew. . . . What must it have been like then for the man I had overgrown into?

A page or two further on, the narrator disconcerts us by achieving a precise objective description of the door at the top of those elusive steps:

> It was a massive green door, encased in summer in a kind of green and white striped housing, with a hole for

the thunderous wrought-iron knocker and a slit for letters, this latter closed to dust, flies and tits by a brass
flap fitted with springs. So much for that description.

The French is even more precise:

> . . . avec un trou par où sortait un marteau de tonnerre
> en fer forgé et une fente correspondant à celle de la
> boîte aux lettres qu'une plaque de cuivre à ressort proté-
> geait de la poussière, des insectes, des mésanges. Et
> voilà.

Descriptions of this kind grow rarer and rarer as Beckett
progresses to and through the trilogy, however. I am not referring only to the descriptions that "self-destruct," like this
one from *Molloy*:

> But would he have come from afar, bare-headed, in
> sand-shoes, smoking a cigar, followed by a pomeranian?
> Did he not seem rather to have issued from the ram-
> parts, after a good dinner, to take his dog and himself
> for a walk, like so many citizens, dreaming and farting,
> when the weather is fine? But was not perhaps in reality
> the cigar a cutty, and were not the sand-shoes boots,
> hob-nailed, dust-whitened, and what prevented the dog
> from being one of those stray dogs that you pick up
> and take in your arms . . . ?

Notoriously, by the time *The Unnamable* is reached, the
Beckett narrator / protagonist has become incapable of affirming or denying any proposition, let alone undertaking a
description of a so-called object, person or scene. There is,
however, another inhibition also at work: Beckett is writing
directly in French. Now, French is an admirable language
with which to describe a door or a table; it is precise, unambiguous. But when one wishes to describe a landscape or

write a lyric poem, ambiguity and imprecision become desirable qualities. The narrative of Jacques Moran, forming the second half of *Molloy*, does not display these qualities — not, at least, in the beginning; it seems but a tissue of clichés. For example:

> Tout était calme. Pas un souffle. Des cheminées de mes voisins la fumée montait droite et bleue.

In the English translation, which is extremely literal at this point, it sounds no more original:

> All was still. Not a breath. From my neighbours' chimneys the smoke rose straight and blue.

Interestingly, as the paragraph turns to the notation of peaceful sounds rather than sights, there are one or two touches that seem to me to avoid cliché, such as "the clicking of mallet on ball" or the "distant lawn-mower":

> Des bruits de tout repos, un cliquetis de maillets et de boules, un râteau dans du sable de grès, une lointaine tondeuse, la cloche de ma chère église. Et des oiseaux bien entendu, merle et grive en tête. . . .

"The bell of my beloved church" and "birds of course, blackbird and thrush . . ." are far too pat, but then Moran at this stage of his life, before his search for Molloy, is the *petit bourgeois* incarnate. What we find in these particular phrases is perhaps not a defect of the French language so much as the unerring ear of Beckett the parodist.

It is the essence of *L'Innommable* that it should reject the eye, and indeed all the organs of sense: even the voice or voices that the Unnamable "hears" in his head do not impinge on any outward ear — or so he believes. What he "sees" as he tries to orientate himself at the opening of the book — Malone, Malone's hat, and so on — may be figments of his imagination, "puppets," as he suggests. But it is hard to write without visual images: the most vivid in *L'Innommable* describe the long shadows cast at sunset by Mahood in his jar and the passers-by on a Paris boulevard. In the pervious chapter, I suggested that much of what Beckett has written about the art of Bram van Velde could be applied to *L'Innommable*, which resembles a traditional novel only to the extent that a semi-abstract painting resembles a work by an Old Master. Instead of an imitation of nature that stands forth complete in itself like a jug or a woman painted by Vermeer, a narrative or a single character presented by Tolstoy or George Eliot, Beckett and Van Velde offer us hints of relationships. But whereas Van Velde deals in this abstract way with spatial relationships, Beckett handles only those that are psychological.

I cannot, however, shake off the impression that in passages of his *Residua* Beckett is challenging the painters on their own ground: that is, he is employing words alone to create visual effects that are akin to those produced by semi-abstract painting. The most striking example, to my mind, is *Bing* (1966). The recurrence of the phrase *blanc sur blanc* ("white on white") recalls the title of a famous abstract composition, but the image presented by Beckett is not in fact wholly geometrical or non-representational; the abstract quality of the scene represented depends on two guiding principles: the limited number of objects presented and the reduction of virtually all color to a uniform white. Quotation of the first quarter of the English translation, *Ping* (1967), will give an idea of the whole, since most of

the elements contained in it are repeated with slight varia-
tions later in the work. From the point at which my quotation ends, Beckett's "translation" diverges farther and farther from the French "original," which itself differs from
nine preceding drafts in French.[1]

PING

All known all white bare white body fixed one yard legs
joined like sewn. Light heat white floor one square yard
never seen. White walls one yard by two white ceiling
one square yard never seen. Bare white body fixed only
the eyes only just. Traces blurs light grey almost white
on white. Hands hanging palms front white feet heels
together right angle. Light heat white planes shining
white bare white body fixed ping fixed elsewhere. Traces
blurs signs no meaning light grey almost white. Bare
white body fixed white on white invisible. Only the eyes
only just light blue almost white. Head haught eyes
light blue almost white silence within. Brief murmurs
only just almost never all known. Traces blurs signs no
meaning light grey almost white. Legs joined like sewn
heels together right angle. Traces alone unover [in-
achevées] given black light grey almost white on white.
Light heat white walls shining white one yard by two.
Bare white body fixed one yard ping fixed elsewhere.
Traces blurs signs no meaning light grey almost white.
White feet toes joined like sewn heels together right
angle invisible. Eyes alone unover given blue light blue almost white. Murmur only just almost never one second
perhaps not alone. Given rose only just bare white body
fixed one yard white on white invisible.

The colors — blue, gray, even black — are all reducible to
white. Furthermore, in the last sentence quoted, "rose" is

an adjective of color, as we can see by referring to the French. (*Donné rose à peine corps nu blanc. . . .* If *rose* were the name of the flower, a feminine adjective, *donnée*, would be required.) "Rose" means the same as "pink" here, of course, and is more easily reducible to white than black is. At the word "ping" in the text, there is always a leap of discontinuity. I visualize the scene as if lit by a series of news photographers' flashlights, making the sound "ping," breaking the continuity, and flooding the natural colors with dazzling whiteness. As the text continues, we suspect that the flashes may be flashes of memory; one of the later images resists reduction to the uniform whiteness: "Ping perhaps not alone one second with image same time a little less dim eye black and white half closed long lashes imploring that much memory almost never."

This passage reminds us that Beckett is not merely content to look out at the world through an artist's eye: one of his favorite images as an artist is that of the human eye. Remember, for example, Murphy gazing into the eyes of Mr. Endon just before his own extinction, "seeing himself stigmatized in those eyes that did not see him; . . ." Although I do not recall his ever actually using the phrase, Beckett unquestionably regards the eyes as the windows of the soul. Murphy's tragedy is partly that he cannot see into Mr. Endon's soul. Remember also the eyes of the girl in *Krapp's Last Tape*, through which Krapp finally is allowed to enter:

> I asked her to look at me and after a few moments —
> (*pause*) — after a few moments she did, but the eyes
> just slits, because of the glare. I bent over her to get
> them in the shadow and they opened. (*Pause. Low.*)
> Let me in.

One would not normally think of looking for visual images in the text of a play, as opposed to the stage directions, but Krapp's reminiscences are in fact crammed with these, whether he is remembering his mother's death — "I was there . . . when the blind went down, one of those dirty brown roller affairs, throwing a ball for a little white dog as chance would have it" — or one of his many women — "What remains of all that misery? A girl in a shabby green coat, on a railway-station platform?" With Beckett, as with most of us probably, memory operates mainly through visual images. Over and over again, he attributes a few of his own most vivid childhood memories to his characters, but in *Krapp's Last Tape*, as Deirdre Bair conclusively demonstrates, he has made use of some of the most poignant memories of his maturity.

As well as receptive, pleading, or merely unseeing, the eye in Beckett can be downright hostile. Alan Schneider writes of *Film*,

> We [Beckett and Schneider] had decided, once the original opening sequence was eliminated, that we would open with a huge menacing close-up of an eye, held as long as possible and then opening to reveal the pupil searching and then focusing — and then cut to Keaton running along the wall. The texture of Buster's own eyelid was beautifully creased and reptilian; he was willing to sit for interminable periods of time, with dozens of lamps blazing at him, for us to get several good shots of his eye, open and closed.[2]

The menace of the eye in *Film* of course lies in the fact that to be is to be perceived, whereas the protagonist is in search of non-being; his flight from being breaks down "in ines-

capability of self-perception." Hence the menacing eye is
his own. At the beginning of the television piece *Eh Joe*,
the camera stresses Joe's similar anxiety to avoid observa-
tion, but just as he is beginning to relax after closing and
covering up the window, the door and the cupboard and
looking under the bed, the Woman's Voice mocks his pre-
cautions:

> Thought of everything? . . . Forgotten nothing? . . .
> You're all right now, eh? No one can see you now . . .
> No one can get at you now . . . Why don't you put
> out that light? . . . There might be a louse watching
> you . . .

It is, if you wish, the voice of conscience, reproaching Joe
for what he did, not to the owner of the voice but to another, more vulnerable woman:

> The green one . . . The narrow one. . . Always pale
> . . . The pale eyes . . . Spirit made light . . . To bor-
> row your expression . . . The way they opened after
> . . . Unique . . .

By the end of the short play the Voice is evoking this girl's
suicide as she lies, semi-conscious from an overdose of sleep-
ing tablets, on a stony beach, waiting for the incoming tide
to cover her:

> Imagine the *eyes* . . . Spiritlight . . . Month of June
> . . . What year of your Lord? . . . *Breasts* in the
> stones . . . And the *hands* . . . Before they go . . .
> *Imagine* the hands . . .

Here again we find an insistence not only on what the inner eye can visualize, remember, imagine, but on the eyes
themselves as an image. The dead girl's eyes are insistently

evoked by the Voice, but it would appear that the most powerful image on the television screen consisted of the huge eyes of Jack MacGowran, who created the part of Joe, staring straight at the camera as it inched slowly towards them. I did not see the B.B.C. production, but a still photograph of MacGowran's face has been widely published.

It would seem reasonable to begin an investigation of the aural qualities in Beckett's work by examining his *Poems in English*, but in fact it is not so easy to escape from an already rather prolonged consideration of visual qualities. To be frank, I find that Beckett the lyric poet has a defective ear. His initial mistake, I think, was to plunge into free verse without first undergoing a thorough apprenticeship to meter and rhyme. To my mind his two best poems in English are "Enueg I" and "Cascando" (not to be confused with the radio play of the same name). Yet even in these there are lines whose rhythm is unalterably prosaic — that is to say, they have the rhythm of *bad* prose. For example,

I trundle along rapidly now on my ruined feet.

Given a natural stress, as above, the line is irredeemable. The alternative seems to be to break it into the heavily accented dimeters that underlie both the earliest Anglo-Saxon alliterative tetrameters and a great deal too much of the verse that is nowadays alleged to be "free," thus:

I trundle along
rapidly now
on my ruined feet.

"Cascando" barely survives its first line,

why not mérely the despaíred of

which leaves the reader wondering whether it is right to give a full stress to "why." If he takes the next two short lines into consideration, he may decide to read as follows:

why not mérely the despaíred of
occásion of
wórdshed

The reader who abandons the poem at this point has my sympathy, but the rest of the work shows strong, unambiguous rhythms that make up for a lack of original imagery and, in places, the absence of any imagery at all:

térrified agáin
of nót lóving
of lóving and nót yóu
of béing lóved and nót by yóu
of knówing nót knowing preténding
preténding

"Enueg I" on the other hand depends heavily on visual imagery, drawn from a particular experience:

Exeo in a spasm
tired of my darling's red sputum
from the Portobello Private Nursing Home

Naming the nursing home so explicitly in that arrhythmic, unscannable line, Beckett forces us to conclude that he is the "I" of the poem and that "my darling" is Peggy Sinclair, dying of tuberculosis. Beckett crosses the high canal

bridge immediately in front of the home and turns right
past the "bright stiff banner" of the advertising hoarding
(now happily no longer there) to walk westwards along the
far bank of the Grand Canal. Almost everything he sees reminds him of blood, wounds, death and decay. The wind
makes "weals" on the surface of the canal; the evening is
"stillborn"; night is a "fungus,"

> The great mushy toadstool,
> green-black,
> oozing up after me,
> soaking up the tattered sky like an ink of pestilence. . . .

Even the human figures in the landscape can be far from
reassuring, although a hurling or football match is described
gaily enough:

> . . . a field on the left went up in a sudden blaze of
> shouting and urgent whistling and scarlet and blue
> ganzies. . . .

More typical is

> . . . a little wearish old man,
> Democritus,
> scuttling along between a crutch and a stick,
> his stump caught up horribly, like a claw, under his
> breech. . . .

As he returns eastwards to the city center from Chapelizod
along the Liffey, "the fingers of the ladders hooked over the
parapet" solicit him to suicide until he sees "a slush of vigi-
lant gulls in the grey spew of the sewer." The final image is

> the banner of meat bleeding
> on the silk of the seas and the arctic flowers
> that do not exist.

These three lines translate a passage in Rimbaud's prose poem "Barbare": "Le pavillon en viande saignante sur la soie des mers et des fleurs arctiques; (elles n'existent pas)." Yet they are appropriate here: "banner" reminds us of the advertising on the hoarding, while "meat bleeding" may describe the sunset as well as "my darling's" lungs.

Strangely, some of the poems that Beckett later wrote in French sound better to me than any of his English poetry, though perhaps they would have less appeal for a true French ear. Although they are again in free verse and in that sense akin to the work of Surrealist French poets like Paul Eluard, these poems do not spring from the free associations of the unconscious mind. On the contrary, they are full of conscious artifice, exploiting antithesis in a way that reminds us of the epigrammatic style of seventeenth- and eighteenth-century French poetry. For example, this brief poem based on the antithesis *like / unlike*:

> elles viennent
> autres et pareilles
> avec chacune c'est autre et c'est pareil
> avec chacune l'absence d'amour est autre
> avec chacune l'absence d'amour est pareille*

In "ainsi a-t-on beau," the antithesis between personal and geological time reminds us more of the fin-de-siècle humor of Jules Laforgue: it is a waste of time to remember the mammoth, the dinotherium, the first kisses, as if it all happened yesterday:

* women come / different and similar / with each it's different and it's similar / with each the absence of love is different / with each the absence of love is similar

> rêver en générations de chênes et oublier son père ses
>   yeux s'il portrait la moustache . . .*

Time eats one up anyway, without appetite. So far, the lines
I have cited appeal to the intellect rather than to the ear.
The next poem, quoted in its entirety, again depends on an
antithesis — perhaps also becoming a synthesis — this time
between Spring and Autumn, but the recurring "i" (and
"y") sounds and the use of alliteration almost force themselves upon the ear:

> vive morte ma seule saison
> lis blancs chrysanthèmes
> nids vifs abandonnés
> boue des feuilles d'avril
> beaux jours gris de givre†

Verlaine's association of *pleurer* ("to cry") with *pleuvoir*
("to rain") is without question relevant to what is perhaps
Beckett's most moving poem, the quatrain anticipating his
mother's death. (In 1948, when it was written, she had already been a victim for some time of Parkinson's disease;
she died in 1950.)

> je voudrais que mon amour meure
> qu'il pleuve sur le cimetière
> et les ruelles où je vais
> pleurant celle qui crut m'aimer‡

* dream in terms of generations of oak trees and forget one's father / his
eyes and whether he had a mustache . . .
† Translated for the sense, not the sound, this becomes "alive dead my
only season / white lilies chrysanthemums / nests abandoned still alive /
mud of April leaves / fine days gray with frost."
‡ Beckett has made his own verse translation, softening the last line into
"mourning the first and last to love me." More literally: "I wish my love
would die / that it would rain on the cemetery / and on the alleys where I
walk / weeping for her who thought she loved me."

Although this poem does not rhyme it is metrically regular.
Each line contains eight syllables according to the classical
rules of French versification. I cannot prove my intuition,
but I have a feeling that in most of his earlier poetry in
French Beckett behaved as though a mute *e* were never
counted as a syllable in verse. At any rate, the poem just
quoted comes the closest to traditional French versification
of all Beckett's work. The content of Beckett's French poems is of the greatest interest, both psychological and philosophical, but it has already been analyzed minutely by Lau-
rence E. Harvey. My concern here is with their form: of the
eighteen poems discussed by Harvey, I have quoted only
four, in whole or in part. There are others I might have
quoted, especially "à elle l'acte calme," which contains the
superlative line

> toute la tardive grace d'une pluie cessant*

but these would only have illustrated the points already
made. In general, then, Beckett's French poems appeal to
the intellect by their logical continuity and their use of antithesis, to the senses by their texture of sound rather than by
any novelty of imagery. The hallmarks of his English poems, on the other hand, are discontinuity and a kaleido-
scopic imagery that is harshly vivid and sometimes highly
original.

In order to master the incredibly difficult task of writing
poetry or literary prose in a foreign language, one must possess what is loosely called "an ear for language." Too often,
this only means a capacity for pastiche or even parody. I
have suggested that one or two lines in Beckett's French po-

---

* all the tardy grace of an ending shower

ems are perilously similar to lines by Verlaine; similarities to Valéry are less close; in view of Beckett's masterly translation of *Zone*, it is almost surprising to find nothing closely resembling the poetic style of Apollinaire. In creating a French prose style for himself, however, Beckett could scarcely help imitating certain models, whether consciously or unconsciously. In a letter to George Reavey he described his reading at the time as including Kant, Descartes, Johnson, Jules Renard, and a French science textbook for children containing sentences like "L'air est partout" and "Le plomb est un métal lourd et tendre." ("The air is everywhere. Lead is a heavy, soft metal.")[3] Did he later consciously imitate in French the style of that textbook? Perhaps not, but his quotations from it remind us of a quality in his French style that has been admirably characterized by Hugh Kenner:

> He is the principal master in our time of the formal declarative sentence, a mastery he has consolidated during his years of writing in French, where one places the subject before the verb and the object after it, and unites modifiers to their substantives with a fragile but inflexible logic. Every such sentence advances the narrative, or the argument, to an exact and measurable degree; there is no ellipsis, no *rubato*, no homely leap of the precipitate heart. The *pace* of this prose is even and indomitable, utterly unrelated to the pace of events.[4]

Kenner forgets to mention that, like the two in Beckett's sample, many of the best declarative sentences are constructed with the verb *être* ("to be"); but Kenner's quotations from *Fin de partie* often illustrate the point he overlooked: "La chose est impossible" or "C'est moins gai que tantôt." Although the verb *être* is not used in the French, the type-sentence of the play takes the form in English of "There are no more bicycle wheels" ("Il n'y a plus de roues de bicyclette"). I do not believe that Beckett's French style — unlike his cast of mind — owes anything to Descartes, but the reference to Jules Renard in the letter is illuminating. Beckett greatly admired Renard's *Journal* and may have learnt something also from the dry, ironic, economical style of Renard's creative work.

Incidentally, the "Johnson" referred to is Dr. Samuel, about whose relations with Mrs. Thrale Beckett once (1937) planned to write a four-act play. Echoes of Johnsonian gravity will be found in the most unexpected places in Beckett's work; the English version of *Molloy* is full of passages that might have appeared in *Rasselas*:

> . . . for my knowledge of men was scant and the meaning of being beyond me.

> And from the poop, poring upon the wave, a sadly rejoicing slave, I follow with my eyes the proud and futile wake. Which, as it bears me from no fatherland away, bears me onward to no shipwreck.

Johnson's conversational style may be recalled on the same page as the second quotation: "I would have been I think an excellent husband, incapable of wearying of my wife and committing adultery only from absent-mindedness." Or is this not rather an echo of Swift? These passages are all, of course, based upon Beckett's French original and lead one to speculate on the French models for the loftier style. Montaigne? Amiel, whom Beckett mentions at least twice in his published criticism? Perhaps the true source, if any, is

Proust, whose work owes something to each and all of his introvert predecessors.

For the extrovert, slangy, obscene passages in the trilogy and for its bitter, eloquent, inexhaustible first-person narrators, the critics seem to have found only one model — Louis-Ferdinand Céline. They may well be right: Peggy Guggenheim said that when she first met Beckett in December 1937 he was full of enthusiasm for Céline's *Voyage au bout de la nuit*. There was, however, another French novelist, Raymond Queneau, who experimented with a colloquial narrative style at the same time as Céline. I wonder if Beckett had not read, say, *Loin de Rueil* and *Pierrot mon ami* before he wrote *Mercier et Camier*. At least two passages from that book capture the humor of Queneau's syntactical games even in English translation. Here is one:

> Have I the honour of addressing the proprietor? said Camier.
> I am the manager, said the manager, since he was the manager.

This type of irrefutably logical statement occurs at least once in virtually every book by Queneau. Another hallmark of his work is the parenthetical comment of the narrator upon his own narration; Beckett offers this example of the device:

> But [the constable] had reckoned without Mercier (who can blame him?) and to his undoing, for Mercier raised his right foot (who could have foreseen it?) and launched it clumsily but with force among the testicles (to call a spade a spade) of the adversary (impossible to miss them).

The violence of this passage is somehow mitigated by its facetious style; Queneau too disguises his infrequent scenes of sudden violence in some highly mannered comic patter: I recall particularly a memorable punch in the face in *Loin de Rueil*, so trickily described that Queneau's American translator never discovered just what was going on! One other French humorous novel, full of bicycles and insults to strangers, may have contributed its mite to *Mercier et Camier — Les Copains* (1913) by Jules Romains. Like Mercier and Camier, the "pals" who give their name to the Romains book are extremely word-conscious, fond of parodying French rhetoric, and rather trying to converse with. Since Beckett did some post-graduate research on "Les Unanimistes," among whom Romains was a leader, he can hardly have failed to read *Les Copains* in the late 1920's, though he may have retained only vague memories of it when he began *Mercier et Camier* nearly twenty years later.

The great aural appeal of certain passages in *En attendant Godot* was recognized from the very beginning. Over and over again the dialogue between Vladimir and Estragon becomes antiphonal, as they exchange brief phrases of similar length and, frequently, identical syntax. One, shortly after the beginning of the second act, has become almost an anthology piece:

v. C'est vrai, nous sommes intarissables.
E. C'est pour ne pas penser.
v. Nous avons des excuses.
E. C'est pour ne pas entendre.
v. Nous avons nos raisons.
E. Toutes les voix mortes.
v. Ça fait un bruit d'ailes.

E. De feuilles.
V. De sable.
E. De feuilles.

Silence.

V. Elles parlent toutes en même temps.
E. Chacune à part soi.

Silence.

V. Plutôt elles chuchotent.
E. Elles murmurent.
V. Elles bruissent.
E. Elles murmurent.

Silence.

V. Que disent-elles?
E. Elles parlent de leur vie.
V. Il ne leur suffit pas d'avoir vécu.
E. Il faut qu'elles en parlent.
V. Il ne leur suffit pas d'être mortes.
E. Ce n'est pas assez.

Silence.

V. Ça fait comme un bruit de plumes.
E. De feuilles.
V. De cendres.
E. De feuilles.

*Long silence.**

Estragon's stubborn repetition of *De feuilles* ("Of leaves")
as the nearest equivalent of the sound of "All the dead

---

* You're right, we're inexhaustible. / It's so we won't think. / We have
that excuse. / It's so we won't hear. / We have our reasons. / All the dead
voices. / They make a noise like wings. / Like leaves. / Like sand. / Like
leaves. / *Silence.* / They all speak at once. / Each one to itself. / *Silence.* /
Rather they whisper. / They rustle. / They murmur. / They rustle. / *Silence.* / What do they say? / They talk about their lives. / To have lived
is not enough for them. / They have to talk about it. / To be dead is not
enough for them. / It is not sufficient. / *Silence.* / They make a noise like
feathers. / Like leaves. / Like ashes. / Like leaves. / *Long silence.*

voices" serves as a refrain to round off both the section before the first silence and the passage as a whole.

The most striking speech in the whole play, Lucky's monologue when ordered to think, rivets our attention at first by its shocking mixture of seeming sense and evident nonsense, mingling reflections on "the existence . . . of a personal God . . . with white beard . . . outside time without extension . . ." with the nonsense syllables "quaquaquaqua." (If God is without extension, how can he be said to have a white beard?) But as an audience loses the thread of the progressively more disrupted sentence, it ceases to try to understand and is swept away by the verbal torrent which, in English, breaks down into the heavily accented dimeters already noted in Beckett's free verse:

> the air the earth
> the sea the earth
> abode of stones
> in the great deeps
> the great cold
> on sea on land
> and in the air
> I resume
> for reasons unknown
> in spite of the tennis
> the facts are there
> but time will tell. . . .

Pozzo's rhetoric on the subject of the approach of night in Act I is clearly an exercise in bathos, but his sudden outburst in the second act is rhetoric of a different order. Part of it would make acceptable free verse in the original French:

Un jour,
ça ne vous suffit pas,
un jour pareil aux autres
il est devenu muet,
un jour
je suis devenu aveugle,
un jour
nous deviendrons sourds,
un jour
nous sommes nés,
un jour
nous mourrons,
le même jour,
le même instant,
ça ne vous suffit pas?*

In most of the stage plays there are set-pieces, such as Hamm's "story" in *Endgame*, to which the audience is expected to listen with special attention; even if they end in anticlimax, these set-pieces are shaped to appeal to the ear. For example, Hamm's meteorological notations, irrelevant as they are to the supposedly pathetic story he is telling, have their crazy symmetry:

It was an extra-ordinarily bitter day, I remember, zero by the thermometer. . . . It was a glorious bright day, I remember, fifty by the heliometer. . . . It was a

---

* One day, is that not enough for you, one day he went dumb, one day I went blind, one day we'll go deaf, one day we were born, one day we shall die, the same day, the same second, is that not enough for you?

> howling wild day, I remember, a hundred by the ane-
> mometer. . . . It was an exceedingly dry day, I remem-
> ber, zero by the hygrometer.

Each sentence is divided into two antithetical parts, separated by "I remember": the first part describes the weather
in vivid layman's language, while the second gives the appropriate meteorological statistic with a pedantry which, instead of clinching the initial statement, makes us doubt
that there ever was a day so perfectly bitter, bright, wild and
dry. The rationalism and balance of these sentences, as very
often in Beckett, have been pushed so far as to seem irrational and unbalanced — to the intellect but not to the en-
chanted ear.

When Beckett turned to writing radio plays at the
prompting of the B.B.C., he naturally wrote in English;
paradoxically, the *language* of these works is less appealing
to the ear than that of either the French stage plays or their
English translations. As in *Film* and *Eh Joe*, Beckett becomes fascinated with the techniques peculiar to the medium: *All That Fall*, his first radio play, runs the whole
gamut of sound effects. First we hear "*Rural sounds. Sheep,
bird, cow, cock, severally, then together.*" At the beginning
and end of the play, the music of Schubert's *Death and the
Maiden* is used; on its second appearance, Mr. Rooney
identifies its title for the benefit of the unschooled among
the radio audience. As Mrs. Rooney makes her painful way
to the station to meet her husband's train, the sound effects
become a sort of history of transport: first, Mrs. Rooney's
dragging steps; then the noises appropriate to a cart drawn
by a horse (or rather by a hinny, offspring of a she-ass and a
stallion), including the wheels grating, the animal neigh-

ing, and the "welts" of a stick or whip on the hinny's rump;
then come the sounds of Mr. Tyler's bicycle, Connolly's
motor-van, Mr. Slocum's limousine, and finally, in the station, both an express train rushing through and Mr. Rooney's suburban train, which halts, lets off its passengers, and
gets under way again. A donkey brays; wind and rain begin;
the final direction to the effects man is *"Tempest of wind
and rain."* Another unusual feature is the Irish English
spoken by the working-class characters. Obviously, Beckett
wants to offer the ear as much variety as possible, but the
dialogue does not include many poetic set-pieces. True,
both Mr. and Mrs. Rooney deliver some long speeches, but
the closest thing to poetry, as I see it, is the long comic
speech by Miss Fitt about her absent-mindedness, both in
church and in everyday living:

> Ah yes, I am distray, very distray, even on week-days.
> Ask Mother, if you do not believe me. Hetty, she says,
> when I start eating my doily instead of the thin bread
> and butter, Hetty, how can you be so distray?

Embers, the second radio play in English, is dominated
by a single sound-effect, the noise of the sea on the shingle,
sometimes loud, sometimes scarcely audible. This is one of
the two strongest impressions created by the play; the other,
strangely enough, is visual not aural. Twice we are presented with a scene in a story that Henry often told himself yet never finished: two old men, Bolton and Holloway,
confront one another; Holloway is a doctor from whom
Bolton wants something Holloway is not prepared to give;
he will give an injection at once, if Bolton insists, but it
seems as though Bolton wants a lethal dose. At one point,

as Bolton pleads mutely, we have yet again the image of an eye:

> Then he suddenly strikes a match, Bolton does, lights a candle, catches it up above his head, walks over and looks Holloway full in the eye. (*Pause.*) Not a word, just the look, the old blue eye, very glassy, lids worn thin, lashes gone, whole thing swimming, and the candle shaking over his head.

Bolton pleads verbally once again with Holloway, who again refuses.

> Candle shaking and guttering all over the place, lower now, old arm tired, takes it in the other hand and holds it high again, that's it, that was always it, night, and the embers cold, and the glim shaking in your old fist, saying, Please! Please!

The word "your," coming as it does in Henry's final monologue, suggests that Bolton is in fact Henry's father, who disappeared for ever as a result of "that evening bathe you took once too often." Was his drowning a suicide, prompted by his disappointment in his only son? Henry lives by the stretch of sea where his father perished, powerless to escape its sound, trying always to evoke his father's presence, to talk to him, yet afraid to ask the one question that would reveal the truth about his death. The final word in the text of *Embers* is the direction "*Sea.*"

It was inevitable, though, that the practice of radio drama would lead Beckett to an exploration — perhaps even to an exploitation — of the great opportunities for the use of music inherent in the form. As we have seen, he had been steeped in music all his life: his cousin John Beckett became a professional pianist and composer; his nephew Edward is now a professional flautist; his wife, Suzanne Dumesnil, was a pianist and music teacher by profession when he first met her. The record of Beckett's direct collaboration with musicians is brief enough, even now, but they have helped him to achieve two of his most moving works, the radio plays *Cascando* and *Words and Music*. This is no accident, because music has always been synonymous with emotion for Beckett. His prose and most of his poetry, even at their most moving, are constantly undercut by irony and parody, but his taste in music, as we have seen, is essentially Romantic: Chopin, Schubert, Beethoven are the composers he prefers to play himself. Mozart, too, he likes, but I can find no reference in his work to Bach. The suspicious attitude towards intellectualism that Beckett developed, slowly and painfully in his own writing and somewhat more rapidly in his criticism of painting, was probably always present in regard to music. The final paragraph of his *Proust*, after saying that "a book could be written on the significance of music in the work of Proust . . .," insists on "the influence of Schopenhauer on this aspect of the Proustian demonstration. . . ." The tone of the following sentences suggests Beckett's fundamental agreement with Schopenhauer, who

> rejects the Leibnitzian view of music as "ocult arithmetic," and in his aesthetics separates it from the other arts, which can only produce the Idea with its concomitant phenomena, whereas music is the Idea itself, unaware of the world of phenomena, existing ideally outside the universe, apprehended not in Space but in Time only. . . . These considerations explain the beautiful convention of the "da capo" as testimony to the

intimate and ineffable nature of an art that is perfectly intelligible and perfectly inexplicable.

Earlier Beckett had quoted "Schopenhauer's definition of the artistic procedure as 'the contemplation of the world independently of the principle of reason.'" And in the place of reason there comes emotion, though Beckett cannot quite bring himself to say so. In *Words and Music*, as we shall see, Music triumphs over Words because feeling, though at first humble and tentative, subverts the pride and hostility of an intellect cut off from feeling, which is in fact no longer capable of offering anything but meaningless formulas.

The first work by Beckett of which original music forms an integral part is *Acte sans paroles I*, written in 1956 and first published in 1957. Beckett's mime for one player may not be performed without the accompanying music, composed by John Beckett.[5] Later, the same composer was to set words instead of movements to music for his cousin, but in the meanwhile Samuel found himself supplying a libretto for Marcel Mihalovici, already a friend of his. When Mihalovici asked Beckett for an opera libretto, he was doubtless unaware of the following passage in *Proust*:

> Thus, by definition, opera is a hideous corruption of this most immaterial of all the arts [i.e. music]: the words of a libretto are to the musical phrase that they particularize what the Vendôme Column, for example, is to the ideal perpendicular.

Holding such views, Beckett unsurprisingly declared that he was incapable of writing a libretto, but he did offer the composer a choice among three French texts as yet un-

published: *Tous ceux qui tombent, La Dernière Bande,* and
another as yet unfinished. Mihalovici promptly chose the
second, translated from *Krapp's Last Tape* by Pierre Leyris
and Beckett, for he saw that "the melancholy poetry which
it releases, as well as its violent eruptions, offered me wonderful opportunities for musical contrast."[6] During fourteen
months of 1959-60, Mihalovici set the complete French
text to music which fills the necessary pauses in the monologue as well as accompanying the words. Beckett finally
stooped to the despised role of librettist in the sense that he
supplied an English text which could be sung to the music;
a German one was provided by Elmar Tophoven. The opera — known in French as *Krapp ou La Dernière Bande,*
and in English as *The Last Tape,* to distinguish it from the
play — was published in Paris in 1961 and has had French
and German performances. Mihalovici has described Beckett as "a remarkable musician . . . he possesses an astonishing musical intuition . . . that I often used in my composition."[7] Elsewhere he has said that Beckett possesses
"un jugement très sûr en musique. . . ."

> I composed the music of *Krapp* under his constant
> supervision, . . . showing him each fragment as it was
> completed: he would approve or disapprove, and I com-
> plied meticulously with his suggestions.[8]

Remembering what Beckett wrote in *Proust* about the
normal relationship between the words of a libretto and
"the musical phrase that they particularize," we might well
have expected that when he came to write a libretto from
scratch, he would achieve something very different from

Napoleon's column in the Place Vendôme. Mihalovici expresses the difference as follows:

> For *Cascando* . . . it was not a matter of a musical commentary on the text but of creating, by musical means, a third character, so to speak, who sometimes intervenes alone, sometimes along with the narrator, without however merely being the accompaniment for him.[9]

So thorough was Beckett in granting autonomy to the music in *Cascando* that, although the work already moves me deeply, I do not feel I have understood it fully on the basis of the words alone. The only clue to the music in the texts available to me — the original French libretto and its English translation — consists of the stage directions *"brève"* (*"brief"*), used twice, and *"faiblissant"* (*"weakening"*), which occurs only once. The comments of the character Ouvreur (*"Opener"*) offer no further guidance, to me at least, concerning the emotional quality of the music. It would therefore be pointless to discuss the play in the present context without having heard one or more performances complete with music. Suffice it to say that *Cascando* (1963) represents Beckett's farthest advance to date beyond the conventional opera libretto. *Words and Music* (1962), with music by John Beckett, is, like *Cascando*, a three-character play, one of whose "characters" is identified simply as Music: in this case, however, Samuel Beckett's stage directions enable the reader to form a clear picture of the emotional content of the music — or at any rate of what the author intended it to be.

Relying on these stage directions — or whatever the correct term is in a radio play — I venture to present a reading of this dramatic poem as it appears without musical accompaniment or even the silent assistance of a printed score — supposing I were able to read one. *Words and Music* seems to me a summing-up of everything that music means to Beckett, his twentieth-century equivalent of an "Ode for St. Cecilia's Day." It well deserves the sub-title Dryden gave to his "Alexander's Feast, or The Power of Music," and recalls the words of his other great ode:

> What passions cannot Music raise and quell?

In Beckett's play, the part of "Music" is taken by a small orchestra, who are heard tuning up as the work begins. Words, a single actor, asks them to be quiet. He seems to detest music: "How much longer cooped up here in the dark? (*With loathing.*) With you!" He then proceeds to give a set speech ("*Rattled off, low,*" says the stage direction) on the theme of sloth. Far from composing it impromptu, as Hugh Kenner suggests, he is rattling off an imperfectly remembered lesson: when he dries up or makes a mistake, he has to go back a few words and start again. The effect is rather similar to that of Lucky's speech in *Waiting for Godot*. Having begun with the statement "Sloth is of all passions the most powerful passion and indeed no passion is more powerful than the passion of sloth," he soon finds that he has forgotten what comes after the definition of passion:

> by passion we are to understand a movement of the soul pursuing or fleeing real or imagined pleasure or pain pleasure or pain real or imagined pleasure or pain. . . .

Finally an old man named Croak shuffles in, begging Words and Music to be friends. "I am late, forgive. (*Pause.*) The face. (*Pause.*) On the stairs." He then assigns Words the theme of love. Words promptly launches on an orotund and more accurate rendering of his pseudo-scholastic analysis of sloth, substituting the word "love" for "sloth" — except for one occasion when he forgets and has to correct himself. Croak finally silences him with violent thumps of his club on the ground and summons Music to discourse on love instead. Music supplies appropriate soft music, over the "*audible groans and protestations*" of Words, until at Croak's orders the music becomes "*fortissimo, all expression gone, drowning* WORDS' *protestations.*" Words is then allowed to launch out on an even more tedious and hair-splitting account of love, asking very rhetorically: "Do we mean love, when we say love? . . . Soul, when we say soul?" Croak, in anguish, interrupts him and urges the orchestra into "*love and soul music, with just audible protestations*" from Words.

Croak then proposes the theme of age, for which Words is clearly unprepared. His faltering improvisation is rejected and Croak demands that Words and Music perform together. At first Words tries to lead Music, but he soon settles down to accept Music's suggestions. After a painful process of composition, line by line, an aria is completed.

MUSIC *Plays air through alone, then invites* WORDS *with opening, pause, invites again and finally accompanies very softly.*
WORDS (*trying to sing, softly*).
       Age is when to a man

> Huddled o'er the ingle
> Shivering for the hag
> To put the pan in the bed
> And bring the toddy
> She comes in the ashes
> Who loved could not be won
> Or won not loved*
> Or some other trouble
> Comes in the ashes
> Like in that old light
> The face in the ashes
> That old starlight
> On the earth again.

After a long pause, Croak proposes "The face." Music makes *"warmly sentimental"* and *"warm"* suggestions, but Words rejects these and gives a cold, rather precise and prosaic account of the face seen by starlight. Actually, the opening phrases are poetic enough:

> Seen from above at such close quarters in that radiance so cold and faint with eyes so dimmed by . . . what had passed, its quite . . . piercing beauty is a little . . .
> *Pause*
> MUSIC   *Renews timidly previous suggestion.*
> WORDS   (*interrupting, violently*). Peace!
> CROAK   My comforts! Be friends!
> *Pause.*
> WORDS   . . . blunted.

Words is clearly in the throes of a genuine improvisation, trying to be faithful to the image in the mind's eye. (I assume that the mind and the memory are Croak's.) The tendency to coldness and prosiness that Words frequently

---

* Compare with the poem "Cascando," above, p. 135.

shows is perhaps justified by the circumstances under which
the face is seen. The young male observer has just experienced orgasm but, "such are the powers of recuperation at
this age," he is soon able to draw back his head and "begin
to feast again" on the woman's face:

> —flare of the black disordered hair as though spread
> wide on water, the brows knitted in a groove suggesting
> pain but simply concentration more likely all things
> considered on some consummate inner process, the eyes
> of course closed in keeping with this. . . .

The description proceeds a little farther; then Croak gives
an anguished cry; "Lily!" Words continues; Croak groans.

WORDS . . . the whole so blanched and still that were it not for
the great white rise and fall of the breasts, spreading as
they mount and then subsiding to their natural . . .
aperture —

MUSIC *Irrepressible burst of spreading and subsiding music
with vain protestations . . . from* WORDS. *Triumph
and conclusion.*

Words resumes, however, and eventually, "such are the
powers —" the pale young face regains its color and the
eyes open. Words speaks *"reverently"* at this point and then
adopts a *"poetic tone."* One is reminded of Krapp's reminiscence, quoted above because of its eye imagery; while the
passage quoted from *Eh Joe* about "the pale eyes. . . . The
way they opened after . . . Unique . . ." now becomes
crystal-clear. Words and Music once again, little by little,
compose an aria, this time describing the penetration of the
woman's eyes by her lover's gaze:

> Then down a little way
> Through the trash

> Towards where
> All dark no begging
> No giving no words
> No sense no need
> Through the scum
> Down a little way
> To whence one glimpse
> Of that wellhead.

Croak, surely overcome by emotion, drops his club and shuffles away out of earshot. The "morose delectation" of remembered bygone sexual encounters has overwhelmed him as it did Krapp. The play ends with Words completely at Music's mercy:

WORDS   Music (*Imploring.*) Music!
          Pause.
MUSIC   *Rap of baton and statement with elements already used
          or wellhead alone.*
          Pause.
WORDS   Again. (*Pause. Imploring.*) Again!
MUSIC   *As before or only very slightly varied.*
          Pause.
WORDS   *Deep sigh.*

                    CURTAIN

What "the wellhead" or *la source*, as it is in French, symbolizes need not, should not, cannot be defined here. Like music, it may be "the Idea itself, unaware of the world of phenomena, existing ideally outside the universe, apprehended not in Space but in Time only. . . ."[10] Even more than *Krapp's Last Tape*, *Words and Music* entitles Beckett to a place beside Proust, the poet of that involuntary memory through whose working we are flooded by a new air and a new perfume (new precisely because already experienced), and we breathe the true air of Paradise, of the only Paradise that is not the dream of a madman, the Paradise that has been lost.[11]

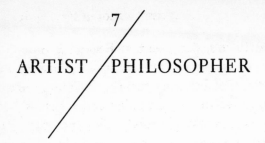

7

ARTIST / PHILOSOPHER

In an interview that he granted with considerable reluctance in 1961, Beckett engaged in the following spirited piece of dialogue with Gabriel d'Aubarède of *Les Nouvelles Littéraires*:

> "Have contemporary philosophers had any influence on your thought?"
> "I never read philosophers."
> "Why not?"
> "I never understand anything they write."
> "All the same, people have wondered if the existentialists' problem of being may afford a key to your works."
> "There's no key or problem. I wouldn't have had any reason to write my novels if I could have expressed their subject in philosophic terms."[1]

The entire interview suggests that Beckett was not in a forthcoming mood; we must also consider the possibility that the interviewer misunderstood or deliberately misrepresented him. Nevertheless, I believe that Beckett is capable, in certain moods, of saying the words attributed to him — more important, of believing them. I am the more willing to accept d'Aubarède as a credible witness because he later quotes Beckett as saying, "*Molloy* and the others came to me the day I became aware of my own folly." The last time I saw Beckett, in April 1973, he said much the same in different words: "I realized that I knew nothing. I sat down in my mother's little house in Ireland ["New Place," to which she moved when "Cooldrinagh" was sold] and began to write *Molloy*."

I think we can take Beckett's word for it that in 1961 he was reading no philosophy and had read none for years. Since d'Aubarède specifically mentioned contemporary philosophers, Beckett may in any case have been referring only to them. When his correspondence is published at some future date, we can hope that it will settle all the vexed questions about whether he read Husserl or Heidegger or Wittgenstein. Jean Onimus has pointed out that Jean-Paul Sartre, Paul Nizan and Maurice Merleau-Ponty were all connected with the Ecole Normale Supérieure in 1928-30 when Beckett lectured in English there, but this alone does not prove that he was familiar with their thinking, either then or later.[2]

What cannot be disputed is that Beckett had read *in* if not *through* the works of some earlier philosophers: *Whoroscope* (1930) is a poem about Descartes; Schopenhauer is quoted in *Proust* (1931) and Descartes' follower Geulincx in *Murphy* (1938); *Film*, written in 1963, begins with Berkeley's maxim *Esse est percipi* ("To be is to be perceived"). David H. Hesla's *The Shape of Chaos* may well be the best guide to Beckett's knowledge of philosophy, surveying not only those philosophers whom he can be proved to have read but also others whose presence seems likely in his work. Hesla is aware of the dangers of this approach and himself issues a warning similar to that implicit in the last sentence of the quotation with which this chapter began:

> In his eagerness to find all the sources and trace all the allusions . . ., the critic may exceed the limits set by evidence, propriety, and plain common sense. Moreover, the critic must go on to show how the ideas work in this or that particular text; but then he stands in danger of accounting for some detail by referring to a doctrine when he could account for it just as well by referring to a technical problem of plot or characterization or emotional tone. (But what is a plot if not a pre-established harmony?) Finally, there are some themes or ideas which have no single source, or whose source Beckett has suppressed, or which he may have developed himself independently of everyone else.[3]

In particular situations there is real danger that, in Hesla's words, "the critic may spend so much time talking about philosophy that he quite loses sight of the artist and his work, and trades his identity as critic for that of historian of ideas." It would be foolish, however, to go to the other extreme and deny that philosophy has any relevance to Beckett's artistic creation at all. I imagine that Beckett, if pressed, would be willing to describe himself, with characteristic modesty, as an amateur in philosophy. One might even be justified in drawing an analogy between his amateurism there and his amateurism in painting. It will be recalled that in "La Peinture des Van Velde" he described himself as *amateur bien sage, tel que les peintres le rêvent:* substitute *les philosophes* for *les peintres* and the formula becomes "a well-behaved amateur, such as philosophers dream of, who arrives with arms dangling and goes off again, arms dangling, his head heavy with what he believes he has caught a glimpse of."*

Beckett has caught a glimpse of many a philosophic theory, but, as he once confessed, "I take no sides. I am interested in the shape of ideas. There is a wonderful sentence in Augustine: 'Do not despair; one of the thieves was saved. Do not presume; one of the thieves was damned.' That sentence has a wonderful shape. It is the shape that matters."[4] Among the other shapely philosophic aphorisms that have delighted him are Democritus of Abdera's "Nothing is more real than nothing" and Geulincx's *Ubi nihil vales ibi nihil velis* ("Want nothing where you are worth nothing"). He appropriates a striking phrase of Spinoza's by substituting *Murphy* for *Deus* in *Amor intellectualis quo Deus se ipsum amat* ("The intellectual love with which God loves himself"). We have already noted his use of Bishop Berkeley's *Esse est percipi*; Descartes' *Cogito ergo sum* ("I think therefore I am") is implicit in much of his work, especially *The Unnamable.*

I don't mean to imply that Beckett's knowledge of philosophy is confined entirely to these familiar tags, preferably in Latin and frequently containing the word *nihil*. (I might have included, by the way, *Nihil in intellectu quod non prius in sensu.*†) I would suggest, however, that he loves to take philosophic wisdom in its tritest, most abstract

---

* See above, p. 113.
† Nothing is in the understanding that was not first in the senses. See above, p. 50.

form — preferably, as it were, fossilized in the gangue of an archaic language — and to flesh it out with the minute particularity indispensable to art. *Film* is, from one point of view, the classic example of this: even an action so apparently trivial and absurd as Buster Keaton's covering of the goldfish bowl to hide the fish's eye becomes a concrete exemplification of the abstract theme *Esse est percipi*. Yet I wonder whether a viewer of the film unfamiliar with the script would ever be able to achieve the necessary feat of abstraction when confronted by all these "demented particulars." Could he ever work back from the eyes of dog, cat, goldfish, God the Father, etc., to the generalizations with which the published film script begins?

GENERAL

Esse est percipi.

All extraneous perception suppressed, animal, human, divine, self-perception maintains in being.

Search of non-being in flight from extraneous perception breaking down in inescapability of self-perception.

Few film-goers, surely, even after seeing *Film* several times, are likely to formulate its underlying concepts with such precision. Even if they do succeed in this daunting task and turn to the printed script for confirmation, they are likely to be outraged by the paragraph immediately following those quoted above:

No truth value attaches to above, regarded as of merely structural and dramatic convenience.

One has to accept that a mind as skeptical as Beckett's will doubt a philosophic axiom like *Esse est percipi* as readily as it will the prophecy of Christ's Second Coming (an example by no means chosen at random). But why, then, exploit the suspect axiom's "merely structural and dramatic convenience"? Well, on the one hand, the artistic end — in this case *Film* — justifies the means; on the other, Beckett was imitating the practice of his master. The true nature and worth of Beckett's discipleship to Joyce are not revealed in his early pastiches of *Finnegans Wake* nor in any of the later limited and controlled linguistic experiments — such as Watt's speeches to Sam — that recall Queneau as well as Joyce. Neither can we find grounds for comparison in Beckett's version of the "stream of consciousness," in essence a soliloquy rather than the multiple awareness created by Joyce, whose stream of language is fed by coenesthesia as well as the more familiar tributaries of the five senses. In form as well as content, Joycean stream of consciousness seems infinitely varied beside the monotony of Beckett's. No, what Beckett learned from Joyce, very early indeed, can be summed up in a single sentence from "Dante . . . Bruno . Vico . . Joyce." After extracting the quintessence of Vico's *Scienza Nuova* in three lucid pages, Beckett coolly states: "This social and historical classification is clearly adapted [*sic*] by Mr. Joyce as a structural convenience — or inconvenience."[5] The words "structural" and "convenience" remained linked in Beckett's mind from 1929 until the writing of the script for *Film* in 1963, over a third of a century later; there is no reason to suppose that the link has been broken in the years since then. Why did the Beckett of 1929 add the parenthesis "or inconvenience"? Probably because he knew that Joyce had an obsessive need — exemplified in the famous "Table" first published in Stuart Gilbert's *James Joyce's Ulysses* —

for an intolerably complicated substructure that might lie concealed below the surface of his work. Also, perhaps, because it is an inconvenient fact that every work of art must have a structure of some kind.

Although Beckett's critical intelligence instantly perceived some of the possibilities latent in the use of philosophic ideas as structural conveniences, his creative imagination did not immediately learn how to make use of this insight. He may never have read *Tristram Shandy*, in which Sterne so firmly grasped the comic narrative possibilities of the "parody of reasonable behaviour" caused by irrelevant associations of ideas. Locke deplored these aberrations, but gave some amusing examples which proved an inspiration to Sterne.[6] *Whoroscope* was based upon the biography of Descartes, not his philosophy; it was not until *Murphy* that Beckett imagined a protagonist who conceived and lived his life deliberately in accordance with certain theories put forward by Descartes and Geulincx. Tristram Shandy and his Uncle Toby, unlike Murphy, exemplified the association theory of Locke without consciously espousing it; Tristram's father, however, knew Locke's doctrine on "clear and distinct ideas."

It is impossible — for me at least — to find the same philosophic unity in *Watt* as there is in *Murphy*, nor is Watt's way of life the product of a conscious choice, as Murphy's at least *seems* to be. Watt is predestined to go to Mr. Knott's house, to stay there, and to leave it again. His experiences result in a profound disorientation, so that his account of them, given to Sam in the third chapter while they are both confined in a psychiatric institution, is, in Hesla's words, "a tale told by a psychotic to a psychotic."

Sam attempts in this chapter to give some idea of the form as well as the content of Watt's communications, which distort language in ways akin to those used by schizophrenics. (Whereas Murphy vainly envied the schizophrenics he nursed, Watt has had the good fortune to be able to join them.) In spite, however, of the many distracting themes — mathematical, psychiatric, linguistic, logical, semantic, ethical — I find two dominant philosophic patterns in *Watt*: one ontological, the other epistemological. Watt at Mr. Knott's house experiences, however dimly, both the difference between being and non-being and the difference between knowing and not-knowing. It seems *a priori* impossible that such negative experience should be communicated, but Beckett's narrator knows exactly how these things are managed in practice — by the philosophic equivalent of sleight of hand or rule of thumb:

> For the only way one can speak of nothing is to speak of it as though it were something, just as the only way one can speak of God is to speak of him as though he were a man, which to be sure he was, in a sense, for a time, and as the only way one can speak of man, even our anthropologists have realized that, is to speak of him as though he were a termite.

The point to remember about poor Watt is that, far from being an aggressive Pyrrhonist, he is not even a conscious skeptic. He wants to believe in whatever he has been taught, whatever is in front of his nose. If an event occurs without a self-evident cause, he doggedly searches for an explanation. The wild humor of many passages in *Watt* depends upon the way in which things, people and ideas — words

even — elude the simple demands made on them by Watt.
Even a pot, in a passage much quoted by commentators,
ceases to be a pot for Watt. Eventually, the narrator and
the reader find themselves participating in this intellectual
equivalent of the clown's stepping on the missing rung of
the ladder. The simplest locutions, the clearest mathematical demonstrations, will not bear cursory examination:

> They then began to look at one another, and much time
> passed before they succeeded in doing so. Not that they
> looked at one another long, no, they had more sense
> than that. But when five men look at one another,
> though in theory only twenty looks are necessary, every
> man looking four times, yet in practice this number is
> seldom sufficient, on account of the multitude of looks
> that go astray. For example, Mr. Fitzwein looks at Mr.
> Magershon on his right. But Mr. Magershon is not look-
> ing at Mr. Fitzwein, on his left, but at Mr. O'Mel-
> don. . . .

At the end of four further pages, the problem has not yet
been fully solved. Perhaps if the narrator had never attempted to solve it, if Watt had been contented with his
pot that was no pot, we should not have been tempted to
laugh; but earnest bewilderment in search of the unattain-
able — the man in the bath with his eyes full of soap trying
to find the towel that he has left in the bedroom — is one of
the saddest, funniest sights known to man or God. The
philosopher's quest for "truth" — a word most contemporary philosophers would not dare to use — or for something
theoretically easier to find, such as an agreed terminology,
is the comic image that underlies many pages of Watt and
gives the book whatever unity it possesses.

The early French fiction that follows *Watt* (the three *Nouvelles, Premier amour, Mercier et Camier*) need not be examined here, since any new philosophic ideas contained in it are developed much more thoroughly in the major works that immediately followed — the trilogy and *Godot*. *Molloy, Malone meurt* and *L'Innommable* attack the problem of being and patrol the frontier between being and non-being with a ferocity unknown to the hesitant Watt. Far from being "of merely structural and dramatic convenience," philosophic ideas are now the heart of the matter: the fictional form becomes a convenience for their presentation. The change to first-person narrative, first used in the *Nouvelles* and *Premier amour*, suggests Beckett's deep personal involvement with his material. In *Murphy* the narrator had often sounded patronizing in his attitude to the title character; the same was true of the narrator in *Watt*, though less often, even after it had been revealed that he was Sam, himself a former psychiatric patient. Still, one must not over-simplify: if Beckett identifies himself completely with Molloy, does he not also identify with the contrasting character of Moran, whose first-person narrative forms the second half of *Molloy*? In *Malone Dies*, the title character struggles to avoid the first person by narrating the life of the supposedly fictional Saposcat-Macmann. As for the Unnamable, he at one stage denies responsibility for his seeming use of the first person — *cette putain de première personne*. Voices in his head may have taken over:

> They say they, speaking of them, to make me think it is I who am speaking. Or I say they, speaking of God knows what, to make me think it is not I who am speaking.

Even in the very last moments of *The Unnamable*, the speaker has not attained authentic being, the unequivocal right to say "I"; worse still, when he does attain it, "it will be the silence" in which he can no longer say anything:

> . . . you must say words, as long as there are any, until they find me, until they say me, . . . perhaps it's done already, perhaps they have said me already, perhaps they have carried me to the threshold of my story, before the door that opens on my story, that would surprise me, if it opens, it will be I, it will be the silence, where I am, I don't know, I'll never know, in the silence you don't know. You must go on, I can't go on, I'll go on.

The reason why the Unnamable cannot achieve true being is surely his inability to make any of those conscious choices through which authenticity is attained according to Sartre's doctrine. Yet the Unnamable exists, however tenuously, by virtue of continuing to speak: "I speak, therefore I am" becomes the equivalent of Descartes' "I think, therefore I am" — even though, as we have seen, the notion that it is "I" who am speaking is sometimes questioned. As Pascal wrote,

> I can certainly imagine a man without hands, feet, or head, for it is only experience teaches us that the head is more necessary than the feet. But I cannot imagine a man without thought; he would be a stone or an animal.*7

The entire trilogy derives an important element of its structure from the paradox inherent in two remarks by Pascal, upon which it offers an extended commentary:

* Note that Malone planned to tell himself stories about a man and woman, an animal, and a stone.

. . . I have often said that the sole cause of man's un-happiness is that he does not know how to stay quietly in his room.

Boredom. Man finds nothing so intolerable as to be in a state of complete rest, without passions, without occupation, without diversion, without effort.
Then he faces his nullity, loneliness, inadequacy, dependence, helplessness, emptiness.
And at once there wells up from the depths of his soul boredom, gloom, depression, chagrin, resentment despair.[8]

Molloy and Malone stay more or less quietly in their rooms because they are too incapacitated to do anything else, yet they do not know *how* to "stay quietly" in the sense of being at peace. The moment they are "in a state of complete rest," all the horrors outlined in the second quotation do indeed well up from the depths of their souls. Had Pascal been a novelist, he might have written the seventeenth-century equivalent of *Malone Dies*. To say this is also to say that Beckett has given the twentieth-century reader something equivalent to Pascal's ethics, though some critics have seen the two writers as most resembling each other in their sense of a hidden God.

If the reader is by now prepared to tolerate the notion that a philosophic theory could be employed as a structural and dramatic convenience, perhaps he can be coaxed a little farther along the same path. Is it not possible that a writer of Beckett's kind could, with the example of Joyce always before him, make use of a theological doctrine in the same way? Without either accepting or rejecting the widespread view that *Waiting for Godot* is a religious allegory, let us consider what problems confront a dramatist who wishes to write a play about waiting — a play which virtually nothing is to happen and yet the audience are to be cajoled into themselves waiting to the bitter-sweet end. Obviously those who wait on stage must wait for something that they and the audience consider extremely important. We are explicitly told that when Godot arrives, so Vladimir and Estragon believe, they will be "saved." An audience possessing even a tenuous acquaintance with Christianity need no further hint: an analogy, they deduce, is being drawn with Christ's Second Coming. They do not have to identify Godot with God; they do, however, need to see the analogy if the play is not to seem hopelessly trivial. In secular terms, salvation can mean the coming of the classless society, that of the Thousand-Year Reich, or any other millennial solution. Ultimately, though, the concept of the Millennium is itself religious in origin, being present in the Old Testament as well as the New; a Jewish audience would remember that they are still awaiting the Messiah.

In other words, a play like *Waiting for Godot* could hardly "work" artistically if it did not invoke the Judaeo-Christian Messianic tradition and its political derivatives. (Having grown up in Ireland at the time of the struggle for independence, Beckett was doubtless aware of the millennial salvationist hope implicit in all nationalist as well as socialist movements.) It is a measure of Beckett's art that he invokes this tradition (this stereotype, almost) stealthily rather than blatantly. His confidence in his own mastery over an audience had not yet reached the level it was to attain in *Endgame* or *Happy Days* or *Play*, however, where all the characters are on stage from the rise of the curtain.

Pozzo, Lucky and the Boy intervene in both acts, so that *Godot* is not in fact a play of such unrelieved waiting as its successors would be. Any critic who accepts the religious analogy sees the boy messenger as equivalent to an angel ("angel" is in any case derived from the Greek word for "messenger"), but Pozzo seems to be a stumbling-block for most of them. He need not be: although Pozzo denies that he is Godot, he tells Vladimir and Estragon that they are "on my land." Other hints suggest that he may be the very person they are waiting for, but, like the Jews confronted with Jesus, they are expecting someone so different that they fail to recognize him. On the other hand, one must admit that Pozzo's treatment of Lucky in Act I resembles the behavior of the God of the Old Testament; it is in Act II that Pozzo himself begins to seem a victim, "a man of sorrows and acquainted with grief." There are moments in the Old Testament when the Jews — or some of them — failed to recognize their God, so we could perhaps argue that Act I represents the Old Testament and Act II the New. But if Vladimir and Estragon represent Christianity rather than Judaism, there are several texts in the New Testament which warn that the Second Coming of Christ will resemble in its stealth that of "a thief in the night." Clearly, I am now engaged in the sort of allegorical interpretation that I earlier rejected; the point is that Beckett has so firmly established his analogy that I am tempted to carry it on into allegory, forgetting that he wrote in *Proust*: "allegory . . . must always fail in the hands of a poet."

Endgame, too, is a play entirely about waiting, in which even less happens than in *Waiting for Godot*. But the principle that something very important has to be waited for applies once more. In this case, the characters are awaiting not so much their own deaths (though these are important enough, to them at least) as the extinction of the human race and indeed of all animal life on earth. *Endgame* is only one of a spate of works of art directly promoted by the existence of first the atomic and then the hydrogen bomb. What makes it unique is that it never mentions these agents of devastation. The zero conditions observed by Clov are simply taken for granted. On closer inspection, the play yields another unique feature, an audacity of a far higher order than the mere omission of the obvious. Where all other works dealing with the *Endgame* situation describes efforts, however futile, to preserve human life or even — in a sharply defined comic sub-species — strenuous measures to repopulate the earth, Clov hurries to kill a flea that might otherwise find a mate and start the cycle of evolution again. When a boy, "a potential procreator," is seen outside the shelter, Hamm and Clov are determined to let him perish. Although very humanly reluctant to die themselves, the pair are dedicated to the philosophic position that the entire human experiment has been a failure and must not be repeated. Other themes are dealt with here and there in *Endgame*, but the underlying monstrous assumption is that the end of the world is at hand — and good riddance! Beckett described the play to Alan Schneider as "mostly depending on the power of the text to claw, more inhuman" than *Waiting for Godot*. Referring to the first French production of *Endgame*, he said that in a small theater, "the hooks went in . . ."[9] Personally, I loathe the play and wonder whether ability to make one's audience suffer is a valid artistic criterion. But it is possible

to concede artistic validity to the play: it can bring about
the "willing suspension of disbelief for the moment" that
in Coleridge's view "constitutes poetic faith." What I
would deny it is any philosophic validity, except in a dialectical process where such a village-atheist oversimplification
is countered by an equally extreme antithetical statement in
favor of the preservation and continuation of human existence on earth. In general, Beckett himself denies the validity of an extreme pessimist attitude to life. As he once said
to me in conversation, "That would be to judge, and we are
not in a position to judge."

The more one thinks about it, the more one realizes how
many of Beckett's other works are also concerned with
waiting, often but not always for death. *Malone Dies* is the
archetype, beginning with the words "I shall soon be quite
dead at last in spite of all"; it is frequently assumed that
death comes to Malone when his hand ceases to write on
the last page, but that is not conclusive, since he might only
have dropped his pencil — it has happened before in the
story — or the pencil lead might have worn away completely
as he had feared earlier. But no, Malone has died more than
a page before his hand stops writing. That, at any rate, is
my interpretation of the phrase "gurgles of outflow" (*glou-
glous de vidange*), which I think refers to the relaxation of
the sphincters at the moment of death. No matter: most
readers are agreed that Malone awaits death and actually
dies. The Unnamable awaits something equally important:
ultimately, no doubt, it is death — but before that he has
to *be*, he has to exist. In *Endgame* being longs for non-
being; conversely, non-being, in the unperson of the Unnamable, yearns for being.

Happy Days is of course yet another play about waiting, about filling in the time before the arrival of eternity — but what if eternity be already here? Winnie certainly is not awaiting death, for death is a thing of the past, as she makes clear in speaking of Willie: "Whereas if you were to die — (*smile*) — to speak in the old style. . . ." She and he may be in Purgatory, though her phrase about the "blaze of hellish light" suggests a less transitory state. Wherever she may be, she does not think, as Hamm does, that "it's time it ended, in the refuge too." (Hamm adds, of course, "And yet I hesitate, I hesitate to . . . to end.") She still possesses what "in the old style" might be called an appetite for life:

> That is what I find so wonderful, that not a day goes by — (*smile*) — to speak in the old style — (*smile off*) — hardly a day, without some addition to one's knowledge, however trifling, the addition I mean, provided one takes the pains. . . . And if for some strange reason no further pains are possible, why then just close the eyes — (*she does so*) — and wait for the day to come — (*opens eyes*) — the happy day to come when flesh melts at so many degrees and the night of the moon has so many hundred hours. (*Pause.*) That is what I find so comforting when I lose heart and envy the brute beast.

In the long run, then, Winnie awaits annihilation and regards the day of its coming as a happy day; "the brute beast," not knowing it will perish, is less fortunate than mankind, appearances to the contrary notwithstanding. In the short run, however, Winnie is waiting, like a Beckettian version of Mr. Micawber, for something to turn up — some snippet of knowledge, some trivial yet unprecedented event, or perhaps just the right moment to sing her song,

the *Merry Widow* waltz that concludes the play. And it
always does turn up: her parasol bursts into flames; Willie,
"dressed to kill," crawls on all fours into her limited field
of vision. Once again she can cry out joyfully, "Oh this *is* a
happy day, this will have been another happy day! (*Pause.*)
So far." *Happy Days* is hardly the antithetical reply to *Endgame* that I demanded, but the two plays do show a dialectical relationship to each other that I fail to find in any
other pair of Beckett's major works. In fact, after seeing the
first New York production of *Endgame*, I turned away in
disgust from Beckett's work as a whole, and it was not until
I read *Oh les beaux jours*, the French translation of *Happy
Days*, in a seminar with Jean-Marie Domenach at the University of Colorado that my interest in Beckett revived, after
a lapse of somewhere between five and ten years.

Whereas Winnie regards total silence as "the wilderness," the Unnamable longs for it; to him, it would mean
the drying-up of all the voices that mutter or shriek within
his head. Some of Beckett's later protagonists share the
same longing. If we can believe the woman's voice in *Eh
Joe*, Joe's main concern is to "strangle" one by one the
voices in his head — "Mental thuggee," he calls the process.
But the voice suggests that this time he may not succeed:

> It stops in the end . . . You stop it in the end . . .
> Imagine if you couldn't . . . Ever think of that? . . .
> If it went on . . . The whisper in your head . . . Me
> whispering at you in your head . . . Things you can't
> catch . . . On and off . . . Till you join us . . . Eh
> Joe?

Henry in *Embers* talks constantly to himself in a vain effort
to drown out the sound of the sea. One might think that all

Henry need do is go to live somewhere away from the coast, but he himself contradicts this: "I'd be talking now no matter where I was, I once went to Switzerland to get away from the cursed thing and never stopped all the time I was there." Waiting and longing for silence are equivalent in the last analysis to waiting and longing for death, but death itself may not be the end. The Unnamable often considers the hideous possibility that he may have lived a life or two already as Mahood or Worm or both. He tries to convince himself that these previous "existences" are mere figments concocted to torture him by the alien voices that provide him with a travesty of consciousness. Yet he can never be sure that he is not in Purgatory, having already lived — or at least in that Ante-Purgatory where Belacqua, Beckett's favorite character from Dante, relives his slothful life in a dream.

I have argued that *Waiting for Godot* employs the idea of the Second Coming as a structural convenience. Purgatory seems to be another theological concept that Beckett has found extremely useful for structural purposes. It formed no part of the Protestant tradition in which he grew up; he may have heard of it first as a doctrine disputed by Protestants, but clearly it was when he came to read Dante that it captured his imagination. "Dante . . . Bruno . Vico . . Joyce" ends with a long paragraph that distinguishes between the purgatories described by Joyce and by Dante: not until near the end of the paragraph do we grasp that life on earth, the endlessly recurring cycle of history, constitutes Purgatory for Joyce in *Finnegans Wake*. From Joyce's Purgatory there is no escape, not even for the individual human being, who dies only to be reborn into the

cycle. Beckett begins the paragraph — a miniature essay —
by insisting on the absence of progress in Joyce's fictional
world:

> A last word about the Purgatories. Dante's is conical
> and consequently implies culmination. Mr. Joyce's is
> spherical and excludes culmination.

Later, he asks and answers a crucial question:

> In what sense, then, is Mr. Joyce's work purgatorial? In
> the absolute absence of the Absolute. Hell is the static
> lifelessness of unrelieved viciousness. Paradise the static
> lifelessness of unrelieved immaculation. Purgatory a
> flood of movement and vitality released by the conjunc-
> tion of these two elements. . . . On this earth that is
> Purgatory, Vice and Virtue — which you may take to
> mean any pair of large contrary human factors — must
> in turn be purged down to spirits of rebelliousness. Then
> the dominant crust of the Vicious or Virtuous sets, re-
> sistance is provided, the explosion duly takes place and
> the machine proceeds. And no more than this; neither
> prize nor penalty; simply a series of stimulants to enable
> the kitten to catch its tail. And the partially purgatorial
> agent? The partially purged.[10]

Beckett's own versions of Purgatory, among which I would
include *How It Is*, *Play* and *The Lost Ones*, are much less
lively than he claims Joyce's to be. Nevertheless, they have
in common with Joyce's Purgatory the exclusion of "culmi-
nation." In Dante's *Purgatorio* the inhabitants wait for
their purgation to be accomplished; in due course they will
climb the mountain of Purgatory to the Terrestrial Paradise
and thence ascend to the true Paradise, Heaven itself. However much they may wish for it, no such happy issue seems
likely for the characters in any of the three Beckett works

I have mentioned. Implicit in *The Lost Ones* is the certainty that no seeker will ever find his lost one and that if there is any end to torment it will come through an entropic cessation of all movement. In *How It Is*, the protagonist comes to the conclusion that his notion of an endless procession of alternating tormentors and victims is "all balls":

> never any procession no nor any journey no never any Pim no nor any Bom no never anyone no only me no answer only me yes . . .

But in that case he is no better off than before:

> so things may change no answer end no answer sink no answer sully the mud no more no answer the dark no answer trouble the peace no more no answer the silence no answer die no answer DIE screams I MAY DIE screams I SHALL DIE screams good

Admittedly this passage is ambiguous, like everything else in the novel, but I think the protagonist has already died: witness his constant references to

> life life the other above in the light said to have been mine on and off no going back up there no question . . .

If he has died already he cannot die again; if he has no tormentor but himself, his purgatorial sufferings must therefore continue forever. As for the three characters in *Play*, all they hope for now is the cessation of the light that focuses on them from time to time and galvanizes them into speech. They *had* expected penitence, atonement, peace. Instead, nothing that they say seems to be relvant, although First Woman keeps hoping that "some day somehow I may tell the truth at last and then no more light at last, for the truth?" But this perfect confession, this perfect contrition,

eludes her; furthermore, when *Play* is repeated in its entirety, she of course finds no new words to say. According
to Christian theologians, a place of eternal torment is properly called Hell. In Beckett's Purgatory, however, as in
Joyce's, we face something worse than pain or penalty: the
meaninglessness of a kitten chasing its tail. Hell is at least
part of God's plan and He knows what goes on there, but a
hideaus doubt occurs to the Man in *Play:* "Am I as much
as . . . being seen?" Since he is unaware of the presence
of the two women, perhaps his world consists of nothing
but himself in his urn and the light mechanically set to continue its cycle of light, half-light and dark through all eternity. In such a predicament, what Beckett called in his
essay on Joyce "the absolute absence of the Absolute" is
given a new and sinister meaning. Philosophically considered, the Man does exist, for he perceives himself; theologi-
cally, however, if his suspicion be correct, he is null and
void: God does not see him.

But Beckett, after all, is not a philosopher or a theo-
logian: he has written a play. When we view the situation
from the perspective of dramatic art, it undergoes a startling change. "Man" is a character in *Play:* more correctly,
he is an actor playing a part in a play. Put yourself in his
place as he stands or kneels ("The sitting posture results in
urns of unacceptable bulk and is not to be considered") in
a property man's simulacrum of an urn, "only one yard
high," unable to move, probably either sweating or chilled,
staring into a spotlight. There are supposed to be people
out there in the auditorium, but with the damned light in
his eyes he can't see a living sinner. Naturally he asks himself "Am I as much as . . . being seen?" In the early days

of *Waiting for Godot*, Beckett had a reputation for emptying theaters, but nowadays the actor can be sure that a small but crowded "house" is watching his starkly illuminated countenance. Not only can he not stir hand or foot, but a general stage direction insists that his face should be *"impassive throughout"* and his voice *"toneless except where an expression is indicated."* He can be described as playing in Beckett's *Play*, but he may be inwardly cursing Beckett for playing with *him* and with dramatic art as a whole.

Beckett always tries to see just how much of the actor's, designer's, director's traditional devices he can do without, but at the same time he demands nothing less than total mastery of their craft from all his stage team. Gradually, the members of the theatrical profession have come to understand this. Having seen relatively or totally unknown actors and directors make their reputations in Beckett, some of the leaders of that profession learned to appreciate the challenge he offers. *Happy Days*, as anyone sufficiently aware of what motivates leading ladies might have foreseen, was Beckett's first play to attract star performers. With the wisdom of hindsight, one wonders how any actress of the caliber of Madeleine Renaud or Peggy Ashcroft could resist the part of Winnie. All Beckett asks her to do is to project essential femininity while immobilized: first from the waist down, with the arms free; then from the neck down and unable to move even the head. Any actress worth her salt believes that, even under the extreme handicaps of Act II, she can still convince an audience not merely that she is a lady — Winnie wears a hat — but that under all that pile of sand she is still a woman.

Nowhere is Beckett more totally the artist than in his

absorbed exploration of the possibilities of a medium. His profoundest research has been given to the infinite potential of the stage play, but let us look for a moment at what he has done in other media. It is well for the television dramatists of today that Beckett was not born thirty years later so that he could have grown up with the medium: in that case he might well have become the supreme master of their craft. As it is, *Eh Joe* seems to me one of his weaker works: Beckett is here discovering not so much the potential of television as that of the "talkie." *Film* is mute but for a single shriek and proves once for all that the possibilities of the silent film are not yet exhausted. In *Eh Joe*, however, Beckett has made no new discoveries: like so many before him, including the makers of TV commercials, he has grasped the potential of the "voice over" technique — but that is all, so far as I can see. As we have already noted in an earlier chapter, the invitation to address himself to radio drama had a remarkable effect on Beckett: if *All That Fall* and *Embers* are not themselves masterpieces, they do point towards *Words and Music* and *Cascando*, which inaugurated a new genre — invisible opera.

Krapp's Last Tape, although a stage play, might appear to be the outstanding example of Beckett's exploitation of a new medium or device. Many people have expressed admiration and surprise at the rumor that when Beckett conceived the play he had not yet seen, let alone operated, a tape-recorder. But in fact a playwright of comparable genius could have written the play eighty years earlier. The classic play about the Edison phonograph might have been called *Krapp's Last Cylinder*, for all the technology necessary was already implicit in Edison's invention — namely, the recording and repeating at will of the human voice. The distinctive feature of the tape-recorder — that it can erase a recording at the will of its owner, thus making room for a new recording — is not made use of by Beckett. The eighty-year lapse during which the dramatic potential of recording machines was not fully exploited suggests that a unique combination of philosopher and artist was required for the task. Many popular works — one thinks of films especially but remembers at least one novel, Graham Greene's *Brighton Rock* — have exploited recordings of voices played after the speakers' deaths. It took a Samuel Beckett to grasp the far greater poignancy in the idea of a living man who listens to the voices of his own earlier selves. Krapp is yet another who is waiting for death, "burning to be gone" or, in French, *brûlant d'en finir* ("burning to get it over with"). The title suggests that he will have his wish, yet there is an ambiguity: "last" can mean "most recent" as well as "ultimate." The speaker in Browning's "My Last Duchess" is already planning to marry his next duchess. The French title, *La Dernière Bande*, is equally ambiguous. Still, one hopes for Krapp's sake that he will be gone before another year is over.

Krapp's comings and goings about his table interrupted a sequence of progressively greater immobilization in Beckett's theater. It began with *Endgame*, where legless Nagg and Nell were confined to dustbins and Hamm to a wheelchair, while even the relatively mobile Clov was stiff-legged. Winnie in *Happy Days* took up where Nagg and Nell left off and revealed that the changes of expression on a human face counteracted the immobility of the head. In *Play*, mobility and flexibility were denied not only to the head but in large part to the voice also; on the other hand, the presence of three persons on stage and the rapid movement of the single spotlight from one to the other counteracted some of the rigidity. The logical next step might have seemed to be a single unadorned head speaking, but Beckett's imagination once again outstripped logic and hit upon a pair of lips as the only visible speaker. From Alan Schneider's conversation and his share in a panel discussion at York University, Toronto, I gained a strong impression that Beckett was first of all intrigued by the technical problem of confining a speaking part to a pair of lips. Could the lips be lit brightly enough to make them visible, at least in a small theater? Yet, but the actress's head would have to remain perfectly immobile for optimum lighting. If I understood Mr. Schneider aright, the very distinguished actress Jessica Tandy permitted herself to be strapped into a sort of dentist's chair backstage, the headpiece of which kept her lips pressed into the aperture through which she spoke. One of the best-known personalities on the English-speaking stage thus allowed her identity to be almost obliterated. Yet this is not as perverse as it may sound: *Not I* is, after all, a play about the denial of identity and one that asserts, with typical Beckettian ambiguity, the very identity that it seeks to deny. Yet again in the case of *Not I* we must acquit Beckett on the charge of perversity, conceding that what seemed at first sight a "gimmick" is in fact integral to the artistic and philosophic unity of the play. Confronted with the completed work, the critic may rightfully wonder which came first — the vision of two disembodied lips speaking or the philosophic concept of a being that refuses to be. Yet even if the artist deigns to settle the question of priority, it soon comes to seem irrelevant. Perhaps, indeed, vision and concept were simultaneous. My diagram of the artist and the philosopher as antithetical to each other does not preclude a synthesis of their roles.

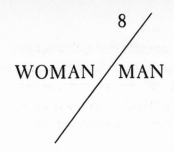

8

WOMAN / MAN

It is typical of the way in which Beckett's reputation has developed, amid an aura of the avant-garde and a critical concern with philosophic abstractions, that little serious attention has been paid to his handling of the relations between the sexes. More excusable is the reluctance to discuss Beckett's portrayal of Woman in aspects other than her relationship with Man, since parts of *Happy Days* and *All That Fall*, the "dramaticule" *Come and Go*, and the almost equally brief *Not I* and *Footfalls* provide virtually all the evidence. Beckett's best-known work, *Waiting for Godot*, not merely has an all-male cast but contains only brief allusions to the very existence of the opposite sex: the longest being Estragon's unfinished story about an Englishman in a brothel. There are other, shorter plays without women characters — *Act Without Words I* and *II*, *Cascando*, *Words and Music*, *Krapp's Last Tape* — but the last two of these are haunted by memories of women. In the rest of the plays, all the novels, and most of the shorter prose pieces, women appear at least briefly, though it might surprise the uninitiated reader to learn that Beckett's first major work, abandoned unfinished, was entitled "A Dream of Fair to Middling Women." On the other hand, the ironic note in that title — a parody of Chaucer's A *Dream of Fair Women* — has prompted the initiated to see more satire and more aggressive hostility in Beckett's view of women than is actually there.

In broad caricature, Beckett's account of the interaction between the sexes may be presented as follows. The woman makes the first advances and will, if necessary, initiate sexual relations. Soon, however, she begins to make emotional demands that the man is unable or unwilling to fulfil. If she is lucky, the physical desire that she has deliberately aroused in him will continue, but even this is all too likely to fade and disappear. Tenderness or any abiding emotional attachment on his part is virtually out of the question. Beckett's male protagonist usually fails to make the most elementary economic provision for his mate — and their offspring, if any — even when, like Murphy, he is fully aware that most other men are industriously earning incomes and providing homes for their families. In spite of this indifference and neglect, Beckett's women remain almost slavishly devoted to their chosen partners. They are given to intense jealousy and — except where they are forced to support their men and themselves by prostitution — to an equally intense fidelity. Usually they bear great physical and mental suffering with stoicism, but if their frustration becomes too great, they are capable of suicide. Celia in *Murphy* is tempted by it; *Eh Joe* describes at length the suicide of one of Joe's women; in *How It Is* the woman referred to as "Pam I think" apparently makes an all-but-successful attempt:

> love birth of love increase decrease death efforts to resuscitate through the arse joint vain through the cunt anew vain jumped from window or fell broken column hospital marguerites lies about mistletoe forgiveness

I assume that this anti-idyll is the male partner's view of the relationship, and that "love" is here equated with his capacity to have an erection, achieve penetration, and proceed to orgasm. A similar equation can be found in Molloy's reminiscence of the elderly woman who "made me acquainted with love":

> She went by the peaceful name of Ruth, I think, but I can't say for certain. Perhaps the name was Edith. She had a hole between her legs, oh not the bunghole I had always imagined, but a slit, and in this I put, or rather she put, my so-called virile member, not without difficulty, and I toiled and moiled until I discharged or gave up trying or was begged by her to stop. A mug's game in my opinion and tiring on top of that, in the long run. But I lent myself to it with a good enough grace, knowing it was love, for she had told me so.

Molloy's grotesquely funny and totally obscene reminiscence continues for a further two pages, during which he worries "whether all my life has been devoid of love or whether I really met with it, in Ruth":

> Perhaps after all she put me in her rectum. A matter of complete indifference to me, I needn't tell you. But is it true love, in the rectum? That's what bothers me sometimes.

Clearly, he isn't bothered at all by his inability to remember whether his *inamorata's* name was Ruth or Edith — or Helen or Penelope, for that matter. The concept of true love as involving the mutual response of two unique personalities is totally foreign to Beckett's anti-heroes, with their "Pam I think" and "Ruth, I think," their confusion of Marguerite and Madeleine. That hallmark of uniqueness, one's baptismal name, means nothing to them, perhaps because they lack one themselves.

I must insist, however, that the generalizations I have been making about the relations between the sexes in Beckett's work constitute, as already stated, no more than a broad caricature, one that too neatly fits the stereotype of Beckett as a thinker imprisoned within a narrowly pessimistic world-view. When, recalling that Beckett is not in fact a philosopher but an artist, one looks at the individual work of art, the dangers inherent in all critical generalization become evident. Every male or female character in Beckett's work differs subtly from every other, and, *a fortiori*, every man-woman relationship is also different from all others. Whatever beliefs Beckett the man may claim to hold, whatever hypotheses Beckett the philosopher (entirely self-taught) may propose, Beckett the artist reveals that life and love are infinitely complex matters.

Look for instance at *Endgame*, that quintessence of despair in which, when Clov finds a flea, Hamm cries out, very perturbed, "But humanity might start from there all over again! Catch him, for the love of God!" The love of God is precisely what is absent from this play; so, one might assume, is love between man and woman. Yet Nagg and Nell in their ashcans, unable even to kiss, feel tenderness for each other. When Nagg awakens Nell, she calls him "my pet" and asks is it time for love; they try to kiss, fail, try to look at each other, can barely see. Nagg, with a generosity admittedly untypical of Beckett's males, has saved Nell three-quarters of his biscuit; when she refuses to eat it, he promises to keep it for her. He insists on telling her "the story of the tailor" to cheer her up. She remembers being happy on their honeymoon; if she does not respond more gratefully to Nagg's offers of food and entertainment, it is because she is at the point of death, as we soon discover. When she is dead, Nagg weeps for her. Of the six relationships possible among four people, those between Hamm and Clov and Hamm and Nagg consist of mutual hostility; those between Hamm and Nell, Clov and Nagg, Clov and Nell, of mutual indifference; only the sixth, that between Nagg and Nell, amounts to love. As Didi said of a much higher figure, "It's a reasonable percentage." Reasonable enough, at any rate, for the mutual feeling of these moribund amputees to redeem *Endgame* from total pessimism and provide sufficient *chiaro* among the *oscuro* to make it a viable work of art.

I cannot help being shocked by Molloy's *reductio* of love, but the more it shocks me, I find, the more ridiculous does it make Molloy appear. The unnamed protagonist of *Premier amour (First Love)* shocks me in a different way: although his physical desire is minimal — less even than Molloy's — I recognize that he knows how it feels to be in love. What I find shocking are first of all his grotesque expression of his feelings and then his totally ungrateful and ungracious treatment of Lulu, who inspired his love and was faithful to him in her fashion. One quotation should be more than ample to illustrate the first point:

> Yes, I loved her, it's the name I gave, still give alas, to what I was doing then. I had nothing to go by, having never loved before, but of course had heard of the thing, at home, in school, in brothel and at church, and read romances, in prose and verse, under the guidance of my tutor, in six or seven languages, both dead and living, in which it was handled at length. I was therefore in a position, in spite of all, to put a label on what I was about when I found myself inscribing the letters of Lulu in an old heifer pat or flat on my face under the moon trying to tear up the nettles by the roots.

Like Molloy, he indulges in the casuistry of love:

> But what kind of love was this, exactly? Love-passion? Somehow I think not. That's the priapic one, is it not? . . . Perhaps I loved her with a platonic love? But somehow I think not. Would I have been tracing her name in old cowshit if my love had been pure and disinterested? . . . Come now! My thoughts were all of Lulu, if that doesn't give you some idea nothing will.

But as soon as he moves in with Lulu, his love for her begins to wane. Away from her, he could think only of her; with her, he can once again concentrate on himself and "come alive in his mind" — less completely than Murphy but somewhat in his manner. Lulu more or less rapes him in his sleep the first night, but after that he compels her to keep her distance. "She could not always resist the temptation to speak to me, but on the whole gave me no cause to complain," he relates with cold, unconscious callousness. She earns a living for them both by prostitution; when he

becomes aware of this, he threatens to leave unless the
clients make less noise. As his account proceeds, the reader
of Beckett's English translation of his own French becomes
more and more aware of the Swiftian tone — one that poses
as a lack of tone, emphatic by the very absence of emphasis:

> One day she had the impudence to announce she was
> with child, and four or five months gone into the bar-
> gain, by me of all people! She offered me a side view of
> her belly. She even undressed, no doubt to prove she
> wasn't hiding a cushion under her skirt, and then of
> course for the pure pleasure of undressing. Perhaps it's
> just wind, I said, by way of consolation.

He vainly urges her to have an abortion; finally, as the child
is being born, her cries drive him from the house for good.
But he cannot escape their ringing in his ears:

> For years I thought they would cease. Now I don't think
> so any more. I could have done with other loves per-
> haps. But there it is, either you love or you don't.

It was the woman's singing that had haunted him before,
just as her cries do now, so that his "thoughts were all of
Lulu." Clearly his love was neither priapic nor disinterested:
it was an obsession from which he sought to free himself at
whatever cost to its object. His self-centeredness is even
greater than Murphy's, although Murphy's love for Celia
seems purely physical.

The fact that *Premier amour*, completed in 1945, was
withheld from publication for twenty-five years and did not
appear in English translation until three years after that
makes me wonder whether Beckett was not himself ap-
palled by his own creation. There are passages of equal callousness in his novels, but we have time in these longer

works to learn compassion for or even sympathy with Molloy or the protagonist of *How It Is*. Yet after I had re-read *First Love*, noting first the hints of eighteenth-century diction and then the overall Swiftian tone, I began to think of the much-disputed ending to *Gulliver's Travels*, after Gulliver has returned from the land of the Houyhnhnms. On one level, Gulliver's disgust with the female Yahoo he has married and his preference for the smell and company of his horses are themselves disgusting; on another level, they are hilarious examples of the absurd lengths to which "enthusiasm" in its pejorative eighteenth-century sense can carry a man. Finally, one comes to realize the sheer delight felt by Swift in pushing a situation and a chain of reasoning to their logical conclusions. This delight in going to extremes is present in all humor and satire, but it seems especially dear to the Anglo-Irish mind — and not always in humorous contexts, either. Swift, Berkeley, Wilde, Shaw and Synge all provide examples before Beckett.

First Love, then, is on one level an indulgence in exaggeration for its own sake, a virtuoso performance. Nobody who has read widely in Beckett, however, can fail to see that it also expresses, in its most extreme form, a recurrent theme:

> Man's love is of man's life a thing apart,
> 'Tis woman's whole existence. . . .

Byron might have laughed over the form given to this thought in *First Love*, but even he could never have included the following in his own published work:

> But man is still today, at the age of twenty-five, at the mercy of an erection, physically too, from time to time,

it's the common lot, even I was not immune, if that
may be called an erection. It did not escape her naturally, women smell a rigid phallus ten miles away and
wonder, How on earth did he spot me from there?

The narrator's near-impotence sets this passage apart from
the stag-magazine stereotype of the man who only wants
One Thing and will go to almost any lengths to ensure that
he continues to get It. For such virility, we have to look to
Man, the only male character in *Play*. First Woman (probably his wife) speaks of "his horror of the merely Platonic
thing," while Second Woman (presumably his mistress)
says, "And of course with him no danger of the . . . spiritual thing." Both women, therefore, are bitterly jealous of
each other. Man is unable to give up either of them and so
is forced to lie, telling each that he has parted from the
other. Of First Woman he says, "I took her in my arms
and swore I could not live without her. I meant it, what is
more. Yes, I am sure I did." Similarly with Second
Woman: "I took her in my arms and said I could not go on
living without her. I don't believe I could have." He did
not, then, in fact live without her: presumably he committed suicide. "Finally it was all too much. I simply could no
longer —" We never learn whether keeping up the double
deception had exhausted him psychologically or physically,
but his final regrets seem to belie the latter alternative:

To think we were never together.

Never woke together, on a May morning, the first to
wake to wake the other two. Then in a little dinghy —

A little dinghy, on the river, I resting on my oars, they
lolling on pillows in the stern . . . sheets. Drifting.
Such fantasies.

It should be noted that the women characters in *Play*, contrary to an earlier generalization of mine, are no more given to self-sacrifice than Man is. "God what vermin women," he says at one point, not unjustly, referring specially to First Woman. The speeches in which each of the three characters expresses pity for the other two, believing them to be still alive and together, need not be taken too literally. Read carefully, these turn out to be expressions of contempt rather than pity, provoked by jealousy rather than compassion.

The title character of *Eh Joe* is the most cruel to his women of all Beckett's *dramatis personae*: he drives them to suicide and then, by an effort of will that he calls "mental thuggee," forgets them. Except, of course, the woman whose voice permeates his consciousness throughout this short television play. Where Joe tries to forget and fails, Krapp of *Krapp's Last Tape* plans to remember but often forgets. His forgetfulness at first seems indicative of his self-centered nature, his ultimate indifference to those who have shared his life. True, he has preserved some of his memories on tape, but as he reads from his "ledger" a summary of the recording made on his thirty-ninth birthday, we are chiefly impressed by how much he has forgotten:

> (*He peers at ledger, reads entry at foot of page.*) Mother at rest at last . . . Hm . . . The black ball . . . (*He raises his head, stares blankly front. Puzzled.*) Black ball? . . . (*He peers again at ledger, reads.*) The dark nurse . . . (*He raises his head, broods, peers again at ledger, reads.*) Slight improvement in bowel condition . . . Hm . . . Memorable . . . what? (*He peers closer.*) Equinox, memorable equinox. (*He raises his head, stares*

> *blankly front. Puzzled.*) Memorable equinox? . . .
> (*Pause. He shrugs his shoulders, peers again at ledger,
> reads.*) Farewell to — (*he turns the page*) — love.

The humor and pathos of the last phrase can only be
brought out fully in performance. "Farewell to —" is doubtless intended to be followed by the agonizingly slow efforts
of an old man to separate one page from the next and turn
over. Whether the word "love" is then spoken in a surprised
tone will depend on the actor's interpretation. A non-
committal tone might be even more comic.

When the summarized tape is finally played, our impression of Krapp's forgetful indifference is reinforced by the
discovery that the black ball was what he clutched in his
hand during the first moments after his mother's death: "I
shall feel it, in my hand, until my dying day." But Krapp
has also forgotten incidents that concern himself only: the
not-so-memorable equinox was in fact the March night
that revealed to him what his life-work would be. Finally,
as he hurries the tape on past this episode, cursing at delays,
we understand that he has not entirely forgotten his "farewell to love"; on the contrary, it is the part of the tape that
most interests him. In his haste, he cuts into the love scene
too far along; after listening to what remains, he reverses
the tape and listens again to the passage from an earlier
point. As the tape evokes Krapp and a girl drifting in a punt
on a lake, one becomes certain that Krapp's definition of
love bears little resemblance to Molloy's:

> I said again I thought it was hopeless and no good going
> on, and she agreed, without opening her eyes. (*Pause.*)
> I asked her to look at me and after a few moments —
> (*pause*) — after a few moments she did, but the eyes

just slits because of the glare. I bent over her to get them in the shadow and they opened. (*Pause. Low.*) Let me in.

This last sentence is ambiguous in English. It might be a plea, either to be let into the depths of her being through the eyes or, more coarsely, for sexual acquiescence. In fact, as the French translation shows, it is a continuation of the narrative. For "Let me in" the French reads "M'ont laissé entrer" ("[The eyes] let me in"). Krapp's love for this un-named girl without doubt includes a spiritual element as well as a physical one.

Not all Krapp's relationships are equally romantic, but it is worth noting that, except for a brief reference to his father's last illness, all his recollections of human contacts concern women. Old Miss McGlome, who sings songs of her girlhood every night, is characterized as a wonderful woman, even though it is "hard to think of her as a girl." The next woman we hear of is recalled from a tape made in Krapp's twenties:

> At that time I think I was still living on and off with Bianca in Kedar Street. Well out of that, Jesus yes! Hopeless business. (*Pause.*) Not much about her, apart from a tribute to her eyes. Very warm. I suddenly saw them again. (*Pause.*) Incomparable! (*Pause.*) Ah well . . .

A little later he asks:

> What remains of all that misery? A girl in a shabby green coat, on a railway-station platform? No?

Next comes a memory of "the house on the canal where mother lay a-dying, in the late autumn, after her long vidu-

ity. . . ." Krapp at sixty-nine seems more interested in the
word "viduity" than in the reaction of his thirty-nine-
year-old self to their mother's passing. The younger Krapp
recalls the "bench by the weir from where I could see her
window. There I sat, in the biting wind, wishing she were
gone." When he sees the blind on her window go down as
a signal of her death, however, he seems moved enough:
otherwise why should he say that he will feel the "small,
old, black, hard, solid rubber ball" in his hand until his own
dying day?

During his vigils on the bench, Krapp sees "the dark
nurse" or, rather, nursemaid: for the third time he is fascinated by a woman's eyes:

> One dark young beauty I recollect particularly, all white
> and starch, incomparable bosom with a big black
> hooded perambulator, most funereal thing. Whenever I
> looked in her direction she had her eyes on me. And yet
> when I was bold enough to speak to her—not having
> been introduced — she threatened to call a policeman.
> As if I had designs on her virtue! (*Laugh. Pause.*) The
> face she had! The eyes! Like . . . (*hesitates*) . . .
> chrysolite! (*Pause.*) Ah well . . .

When the older Krapp starts to record his last tape, he is
full of scorn for his younger self, who missed the opportunity
of a lifetime — not the nursemaid, but the girl in the punt
whose eyes let him in:

> The eyes she had! . . . Everything there, everything on
> this old muckball, all the light and dark and famine
> and feasting of . . . (*hesitates*) . . . the ages! (*In a
> shout.*) Yes! (*Pause.*) Let that go! Jesus! Take his mind
> off his homework! Jesus! (*Pause. Weary.*) Ah well,
> maybe he was right. (*Pause.*) Maybe he was right.

Krapp had clearly broken off with this girl for fear she would distract him from the composition of "the opus . . . magnum" now contemptuously referred to as "his home-work." Two further women are evoked before Krapp throws away his last tape in disgust. The first is the heroine of Theodor Fontane's *Effi Briest*: "Scalded the eyes out of me reading *Effie* [*sic*] again, a page a day, with tears again." Krapp imagines he could have been happy with Effie, but his thoughts switch to a totally different kind of woman:

> Fanny came in a couple of times. Bony old ghost of a whore. Couldn't do much, but I suppose better than a kick in the crutch. The last time wasn't so bad. How do you manage it, she said, at your age? I told her I'd been saving up for her all my life.

The last words recorded on the last tape, however, are "Lie down across her" — an evocation of the girl in the punt. Then, for the third time, Krapp plays the love passage from the tape made on his thirty-ninth birthday:

> I lay down across her with my face in her breasts and my hand on her. We lay there without moving. But under us all moved, and moved us, gently, up and down, and from side to side.

After this, we hear for the first time the ironic closing words of this tape:

> Perhaps my best years are gone. When there was a chance of happiness. But I wouldn't want them back. Not with the fire in me now. No, I wouldn't want them back.

As Krapp sits motionless, staring before him while the cur-tain falls, the audience, despite all the play's ambiguities,

must be convinced that he *does* want those years back —
would want them back even if his "great work" had won a
Nobel Prize.

Krapp's Last Tape, for all its brevity and its many ironies,
is one of the most deeply moving works in the modern theater — deeply moving in a most traditional way. If such a
monologue had been based on Edison's first phonograph,
the Victorians — who loved monologues — would have
wallowed in its sentiment. When Krapp proclaimed that
"all the light and dark and famine and feasting . . . of the
ages" were to be found in a woman's eyes, the audience
would have burst into spontaneous applause, though one
doubts if Sir Henry Irving or any of his rivals could have
been persuaded to put on Krapp's clown make-up (*"White
face. Purple nose."*). Yet a Victorian audience would be
fully aware that Krapp might in the long run have said of
his affair with the girl in the punt what he said of his affair
with Bianca: "Well out of that, Jesus yes!" Obviously, it is
only while a man is still in love with a woman that the light
and dark, etc., seem to dwell in her eyes. Krapp has been in
love, is still in love to the extent that he continues to feel
this selfless admiration for another human being, but at the
time when he broke off relations with the girl in the punt,
he obviously valued his own future success more highly
than her love.

Beckett perhaps allows Krapp to give exaggerated expression to real feeling in the passage "Everything
there . . ." or the very Irish hyperbole of "Scalded the eyes
out of me . . . ," just as he permits Molloy or the absurd
protagonist of *First Love* to exaggerate his lack of traditional emotion. We have no right to identify Beckett

wholly either with Krapp or with the two abject figures just mentioned. What we *are* entitled to say is that a writer who can present both attitudes to love with equal conviction must be a very great artist indeed. That he may also be a deeply divided personality is his concern, not ours. Actually, Krapp and the anti-hero of *First Love* do not represent polar extremes: they are both capable of escaping from the prison of Self long enough to recognize and become obsessed with the existence of an Other. Both, however, strive to abort their love, whether in the name of a slothful "peace" or that of an illusory great work to be accomplished. Their true polar opposites are all those solitary anti-heroes — Watt, Molloy, Malone, Macmann, the Unnamable — who seem incapable of love from the start: their physical impotence, like Belacqua's in *More Pricks Than Kicks*, symbolizes their emotional sterility.

An author who has written so frequently — and at times, one feels, compulsively — about the inability to love must have suspected that he himself was incapable of this emotion or at least doubted that he had in fact ever experienced the unselfish devotion that both the moralist and the artist have agreed to call true love. But does any man, particularly one so sensitive and introspective as Beckett, ever feel that he has loved *enough*, that his emotion was ever totally free from the taint of self-regard? At any rate, as Beckett has grown older, his view of the relationships between men and women has grown less one-sided, though perhaps no other male character shows the range of feeling present in the brutally misnamed Krapp, unless it be Croak of *Words and Music*, the bearer of an almost equally unpalatable surname. "Krapp" and "Croak" are, like "Grock," clownish names: Beckett is so terrified of insincerity, of sentimentality, of cliché, that he cannot present deep and sincere emotion without pretending to laugh at it by the use of such rather mechanical comic devices. The tape-recorder in *Krapp's Last Tape* is itself literally a mechanical comic device. The most extraordinary fact about this play is not that such profound emotion comes squawking out of the machine: that is just what we might expect of Beckett. No, it is when Krapp *in his own voice* strikes an even deeper tone as he records his last tape that the play reaches a climax so free of subterfuge that no later anticlimax can destroy it.

A man learns his attitude to women in the first place from his relationship with his own mother. It must be confessed that Beckett's women feel, or at any rate show, very little love for their offspring, when they have any. The only Beckett character to have a profound — though troubled — relationship with either parent is Henry in *Embers*, who talks endlessly to his dead father. Hamm in *Endgame* says he was a father to Clov, but it is implied that he took over the role in the absence of Clov's natural father. And a miserable father-substitute he has made: Clov has never to his own knowledge had an instant of happiness, though he believes that if he could kill Hamm he would die happy. Relations between natural father and natural son are equally bad, however. Hamm calls Nagg "accursed progenitor" and "accursed fornicator." Again:

HAMM   Scoundrel! Why did you engender me?
NAGG   I didn't know.
HAMM   What? What didn't you know?
NAGG   That it'd be you.

Later, Nagg admits that Hamm's hostility is natural:

> Whom did you call when you were a tiny boy, and were
> frightened, in the dark? Your mother? No. Me. We let
> you cry. Then we moved you out of earshot, so that we
> might sleep in peace.

Curiously enough, the story that Hamm tries to tell concerns a very different sort of father, one who pleads with
Hamm to give him "bread for his brat" and to take both
father and son into his house. If the story is truth and not
fiction, Clov may be the "brat" in question. Hamm never
addresses Nell — presumably his mother — nor she him: at
best, he is indifferent to her.

Fathers, then, may be protective or threatening figures
for their sons,* but Beckett's mothers never seem adequate,
for either good or evil. The mother of Molloy, for example,
although he spends much of his time traveling home to her,
is described as "that poor old uniparous whore," "this deaf
blind impotent mad old woman," who smells most vilely.
Mother and son communicate, it is true, but it can't be said
that they achieve perfect mutual understanding.

> I got into communication with her by knocking on her
> skull. One knock meant yes, two no, three I don't know,
> four money, five goodbye. I was hard put to ram this
> code into her ruined and frantic understanding, but I
> did it, in the end. That she should confuse yes, no,
> I don't know and goodbye, was all the same to me, I
> confused them myself. But that she should associate
> the four knocks with anything but money was some-
> thing to be avoided at all costs.

She filled a maternal role to the extent that she gave him
money, but any gratitude that he feels is reserved for her
efforts not to become a mother at all:

---

* Compare the relationship between Moran and his son in *Molloy*.

My mother. I don't think too harshly of her. I know
she did all she could not to have me, except of course
the one thing. . . . But it was well-meant and that's
enough for me. No it is not enough for me, but I give
her credit, though she is my mother, for what she tried
to do for me.

The best mother, then, is the one who has no children — an
Irish bull appropriate for a man named Molloy. Maddy
Rooney in *All That Fall* comes closest to this definition.
Whether "Minnie! Little Minnie!" ever lived except in
Mrs. Rooney's imagination is open to doubt; what is certain
is that she does not now exist. "In her forties now she'd be,
I don't know, fifty, girding up her lovely little loins, getting
ready for the change. . . ." Schubert's *Death and the
Maiden*, the musical theme of *All That Fall* — played over
and over on her gramophone by an old woman, "all alone
in that great empty house" — refers to Minnie as well as to
the little girl in Jung's lecture who "had never been really
born" and the little child (sex unspecified) who fell out of
Mr. Rooney's train. Childless Maddy Rooney, "weep[ing]
her heart out on the highways and byways," seems the
tenderest mother in all of Beckett; perhaps she would have
been equally tender-hearted had Minnie lived, but we can't
be sure. I have mentioned elsewhere the passage in which
the protagonist of *How It Is* prays according to his mother's
instructions while her eyes "burn with *severe* love" (my
italics). Only one mother in Beckett is herself seen in
prayer, Saposcat's in *Malone Dies*. Her son is about to take
his university entrance examination:

> Kneeling at her bedside, in her night-dress, she ejacu-
> lated, silently, for her husband would not have ap-

proved, Oh God grant he pass, grant he pass, grant he scrape through!

Poor Mrs. Saposcat has made excuses to her husband for their son's lack of success at school, but it seems likely that, if young Saposcat fails again, her ambition will not allow her to feel much further sympathy for him. The reader is not greatly surprised when Saposcat reappears later on as a social outcast, now known as Macmann. Having received little love in his youth, Macmann is able to give little. His "love" episode in old age, with the yet older Moll, is grotesque in the extreme. As Malone, his creator, writes,

> . . . one can only speculate on what he might have achieved if he had become acquainted with true sexuality at a less advanced age.

A conscientious survery of Beckett's women could hardly begin better than with his first volume of fiction, *More Pricks Than Kicks*, which has the added interest of being founded upon the discarded manuscript of "A Dream of Fair to Middling Women." Although usually considered to be a volume of short stories, *More Pricks Than Kicks* is in fact a novel dealing with the loves, marriages, death and burial of Belacqua Shuah. Only the first and third of the stories, "Dante and the Lobster" and "Ding-Dong," are detachable: each "establishes" the character Belacqua — the first story from inside, the other by means of a narrator — and then presents an anecdote that illuminates his peculiar sensibility. The other eight pieces remain mere chapters from a novel, virtually incomprehensible without some prior sense of the personality of Belacqua. The only possible exception would be "Yellow," which relates the manner of his death. Until the last possible second, the reader, as in "Dante and the Lobster," feels himself firmly located within Belacqua's consciousness and may therefore have no need of any earlier acquaintance with the central character.

Despite the pejorative tone of "fair to middling," Belacqua in fact finds himself surrounded by a bevy of beautiful or near-beautiful women; some are virtuous, some not, but all have strongly marked personalities. In one way or another, Belacqua manages to disappoint them all, even his Italian teacher in "Dante and the Lobster." Although she says, "You make rapid progress," she gently snubs him when he wonders "like a fool" how to translate an untranslatable line of Dante.

Of Winnie, the fair woman in "Fingal," all we need to know is that "she was pretty, hot and witty, in that order." After making love to her twice one Spring morning in the countryside north of Dublin, Belacqua offers a lame excuse to leave her with a doctor friend of hers whom they have just met. Belacqua, "who could on no account resist a bicycle," then steals one and pedals off to an abandoned tower where Swift's Stella once lived. ("That" said Belacqua "is where I have sursum corda.") After entering the tower, he soon re-emerges and departs rapidly on the bicycle; he is last seen that day drinking heavily in a public house in the village of Swords. *Sursum corda* ("Lift up your hearts" in the Anglican prayer book) is Belacqua's euphemism for voyeurism, as we discover in the later story "Walking Out." Intercourse makes him a "sad animal," in Aristotelian phrase, but the more cerebral delights of the voyeur seem to cheer his heart. "Ding-Dong," however, reverses the pattern of the previous story. After delighting

his aesthetic sense with the luminous countenance of the
"woman of the people" and his intellect with her breath-
taking offer of "seats in heaven . . . tuppence apiece, four
fer a tanner," Belacqua, we are told, "also departed, but for
Railway Street, beyond the river." Railway Street is the
present name of Lower Tyrone Street, where Bella Cohen's
brothel was situated according to Joyce's *Ulysses*. The
street's change of name was intended to symbolize a change
of function, but it was notorious in Dublin during the
thirties that one could still find a whore or an illegal after-
hours drink there. Which commodity Belacqua departed in
search of remains, like so much else in Beckett, uncertain.

"The Alba, Belacqua's current one and only," in "A Wet
Night," is without dispute the most attractive woman in
Belacqua's circle of intellectual and would-be-intellectual
acquaintances — "the belle of the ball," in fact. Belacqua
idealized her as "not woman of flesh," despite his vision of
the clown Grock moaning the German equivalent of "no-ot
poss-ssible." After an appalling party given by an appalling
woman known as "the Frica," Alba invites the damp,
bedraggled Belacqua home with her:

> He went in. She would sit in a chair and he would sit
> on the floor at last and her thigh against his baby an-
> thrax would be better than a foment. For the rest, the
> bottle, some natural tears and in what hair he had left
> her high-frequency fingers.
> *Nisscht mööööööglich. . . .*

Grock's cynical phrase, here repeated, suggests that something less platonic went on. In any case, when Belacqua
"came out of Casa Alba in the small hours of the morning,"
he soon experienced "such a belly-ache as he had never

known." This may have been chiefly the result of a heavy
night's drinking, but it hardly seems a chivalrous response
to the Alba's generosity. Was Belacqua disgusted by her
unsuspected carnality?

Winnie in "Fingal" was described as the "last girl he
went with before a memorable fit of laughing incapacitated
him from gallantry for some time. . . ." Even if Belacqua
did not disappoint the Alba, he certainly proves less than
gallant or virile in the stories that succeed "A Wet Night."
In "Love and Lethe" he suggests a suicide pact to the beautiful and intelligent Ruby Tough, who is suffering from an
incurable disease. Only after the suicide weapon goes off
prematurely and harmlessly does Belacqua find something
more constructive to do alone with a young woman on a
mountainside than blowing her brains out. We next find
him engaged to the entrancing Lucy, a fine horsewoman,
whose face and figure arouse carnal raptures in the narrator
of "Walking Out":

> Indeed she was better than lovely . . . with her jet
> of hair and her pale set face, the whipcord knee and the
> hard bust sweating a little inside the black jersey.

Oblivious to these charms, Belacqua constantly urges Lucy
to take a *cicisbeo* and talks "of her living with him like a
music while being the wife in body of another." One evening, just as Belacqua has been caught spying on a pair of
lovers in a pine wood, Lucy's horse is struck by a car and she
herself is crippled for life. As for Belacqua:

> . . . now he is happily married to Lucy and the ques-
> tion of cicisbei does not arise. They sit up to all hours
> playing the gramophone, *An die Musik* is a favourite

with them both, he finds in her big eyes better worlds than this, they never allude to the old days when she had hopes of a place in the sun.

At the beginning of the next story, "What a Misfortune," however, we find that Lucy is dead, "after two years of great physical suffering borne with such fortitude as only women seem able to command. . . ." Belacqua "woke up one fine afternoon to find himself madly in love" again "— a divine frenzy, you understand, none of your lewd passions." His beloved this time bears the grotesque name of Thelma bboggs ("bogs" being Portora slang for "privy"), but she is far from grotesque in appearance, "with intense appeal . . . from the strictly sexual standpoint." The poor girl is destined to a great disappointment, foreshadowed by the title of the story. Beckett had previously published in *T.C.D.: A College Miscellany* a parody of Joyce entitled "Che Sciagura": the reference is to the lament of the eunuch in Voltaire's *Candide*, "Che sciagura d'essere senza coglioni" ("What a misfortune to be without testicles"). One is hardly surprised to learn in "Draff," the last story, that Thelma "perished of sunset and honeymoon that time in Connemara." Incidentally, her real father was probably one Walter Draffin, who intends some day to publish "his *Dream of Fair to Middling Women*, held up in the *limae labor* stage for the past ten or fifteen years."

Belacqua's third and last bride is the Smeraldina: one of her passionate love letters to him, in a mixture of German and illiterate English, makes up the eighth story, "The Smeraldina's Billet Doux." After Belacqua's death, we learn how she achieved the right to be his widow. Shortly after Thelma perished, they suddenly seemed to be all dead, Lucy of course long since, Ruby duly, Winnie to decency, Alba Perdue in the natural course of being seen home. Belacqua looked round and the Smeraldina was the only sail in sight. In next to no time she had made up his mind by not merely loving but wanting him with such quasi-Gorgonesque impatience as her letter precited evinces.

Belacqua's last wife seems to have been content enough: her disappointment began at his untimely death. She quickly consoled herself, however, with Capper ("Hairy") Quin, Belacqua's perennial best man.

More Pricks Than Kicks, considered as a novel, is a very curious work indeed. It might be described as the Beckettian equivalent of Flaubert's *L'Education sentimentale*, a monograph on the love-life of a rather passive and passionless man, but not strictly analogous to Stendhal's *Armance*, whose hero is impotent from the start. One wonders why Belacqua should go to all the trouble of marrying the luckless Lucy or the still more hapless Thelma, if a platonic or voyeuristic satisfaction is what he really desires. At times there seems to be a voyeuristic element in Beckett's own descriptions of his heroines, especially this one of La Smeraldina:

> Bodies don't matter but hers went something like this: big enormous breasts, big breech, Botticelli thighs, knock-knees, square ankles, wobbly, poppata, mammose, slobbery-blubbery, bubbubbubbub, the real button-busting Weib, ripe. Then, perched away high out of sight on top of this porpoise prism, the sweetest little pale Pisanello of a birdface ever.

The book constantly hovers over sexuality, without ever quite alighting and coming to grips with it. The more

nearly obscene passages are shrouded by literary allusions
or, as in the quote from *Le Roman de la rose* in "A Wet
Night," by foreign languages. Belacqua performs his neu-
rotic dance of death with woman after woman, all beautiful
in body and moderately healthy in mind, until he dies himself, more or less accidentally, surrounded by a bevy of attractive and kindly nurses. Ironically, he no longer wishes to
die: we are told in "Ding-Dong" that at some point in his
life "he toed the line and began to relish the world." The
critic of *More Pricks Than Kicks* — and perhaps also its
author, who never wanted it reprinted and has not translated it into French — envies the forthrightness of judgment
shown by the Irish Censorship of Publications Board in
branding it "in general tendency indecent and obscene."*

Celia, in *Murphy*, is yet another of the early Beckett's
beautiful, devoted young women, cruel to Murphy only in
the sense that she wishes him to earn a living so that she
need not go back to prostitution. Murphy's virility, unlike
Belacqua's, is never open to question, at least in Celia's
company. Murphy, it is true, would like to free himself
from *all* bodily desires, but he eventually despairs of achieving this and decides to return to Celia; ironically, death pre-
vents him. Yet more ironically, Celia has learned to understand Murphy in his absence, thanks to her sessions in his
rocking-chair: if he had suceeded in returning to her, she
would no longer have insisted on his earning a living. These
star-crossed lovers (literally so, since Murphy is misguided
by a horoscope) are the only pair in Beckett to achieve complete mutual understanding — after they have in fact
parted for ever.

* See above, p. 38.

But already in *Murphy* the gallery of female grotesques that began with "the Frica" is expanding rapidly. Miss Counihan is a "bitch," but handsome and intelligent; Miss Carridge, however, diffuses an ineradicable body odor, while Miss Rosie Dew, though a gifted medium, suffers from "Duck's disease . . . a distressing pathological condition in which the thighs are suppressed and the buttocks spring directly from behind the knees. . . ." In *Watt*, most of the female members of the "fortunate family" named Lynch suffer from incurable diseases: for example, the younger Ann, "whose it will be learnt with great regret beauty and utility were greatly diminished by two withered arms and a game leg of unsuspected tubercular origin. . . ." In this novel, too, we find the first of the series of grotesque love affairs which culminates in the aged Macmann's *passade* with the dying Moll, she whose last remaining tooth is carved in the form of a crucifix. Watt's lady-love is the fishwoman Mrs. Gorman, "of an advanced age and by nature also denied those properties that attract men to women. . . ." Of their love-making, we learn that it consisted of sitting in each other's laps and kissing; "Mrs. Gorman did not always sit on Watt, for sometimes Watt sat on Mrs. Gorman." As for any fuller consummation, "Watt had not the strength, and Mrs. Gorman had not the time." Molloy, we have seen, came closer to knowing "true love," but it is Macmann and Moll in *Malone Dies* who reach the pinnacle of grotesque ecstasy. Their copulations, it is true, result only in "a kind of sombre gratification," but this in turn inspires the love-letters of Moll and the verses of "Hairy" Macmann — forms of self-expression that veer hilariously from the elegiac to the obscene.

In *The Unnamable* too there is a love affair, the strangest of all. Worm, "speechless" and having "lost all [his] members with the exception of the onetime virile," finds himself in Paris, "stuck like a sheaf of flowers in a deep jar, its neck flush with my mouth, on the side of a quiet street near the shambles. . . ." Here he is cared for by the proprietress of the chop-house across the way, who, once a week, feeds him and takes away his waste products for her kitchen-garden. At first he thinks that her motives are purely utilitarian:

> For quite apart from the services I rendered to her lettuce, I constituted for her establishment a kind of landmark, not to say an advertisement. . . . Yes, I represent for her a tidy little capital and, if I should ever happen to die, I am convinced she would be genuinely annoyed.

Later, because of "the redoubled attentions she has been lavishing on me for some time past," Worm concludes that this woman — whom he calls either Marguerite or Madeleine indifferently — "is losing faith in me"; this in turn causes him to lose his always meager faith in his own existence:

> That the jar is really standing where they say, all right, I wouldn't dream of denying it. . . . No, I merely doubt that I am in it. It is easier to raise a shrine than to bring the deity down to haunt it. . . . No matter. She loves me, I've always felt it. She needs me. Her chop-house, her husband, her children if she has any, are not enough, there is in her a void that I alone can fill. It is not surprising then she should have visions.

It will be objected that the reader is not supposed to give any credence to this episode: Beckett is exploring the na-

ture of non-existence; both Worm and Madeleine-
Marguerite are products of the Unnamable's "voices,"
which try to trick him into believing that he exists. True,
but may we not still admire the power of Beckett's imagination, which creates a strangely human relationship between
an imaginary woman and the abortive product of her fan-
tasy? Once again in Beckett feminine devotion is the substance, its unworthy, barely masculine object the shadow.

The two profoundest studies of this feminine devotion,
however, are *All That Fall* and *Happy Days*. It is no accident, I'm sure, that both these plays, like *Krapp's Last
Tape*, were written in Beckett's mother-tongue and only
later rendered into French. Beckett wrote to Alan Schneider that the translation of *Fin de partie* "will inevitably be
a poor substitute for the original (the loss will be much
greater than from the French to the English 'Godot'). . . ."[1] Actually, most of the cold cruelty of the
French does survive in *Endgame*, but the tenderness and
poetry of the three English plays just mentioned are diminished in French translation.

Maddy Rooney of *All That Fall* bears more resemblance
to Winnie of *Happy Days* than may appear at first sight.
Certainly they are both talkative, childless, and married to
unrewarding husbands, but there is a big difference between their ages and also between their temperaments.
Maddy is "in her seventies," Winnie only "about fifty."
Maddy rails constantly against her lot, weeps, sobs aloud,
speaks brokenly, explodes in anger, laughs wildly. Winnie,
on the other hand, shows great restraint, as a rule: sometimes her voice breaks, sometimes she is vehement or disgusted, but she never laments her situation; instead she

speaks of "great mercies" or remarks, "That is what I find so wonderful. . . ." Broadly speaking, Winnie is a stoic and even at times an optimist, while Maddy on the whole is a pessimist. Some of the apparent differences between them, however, are the result of a difference in medium. Because *All That Fall* is a play for radio, the tone of Maddy's voice is the only sure guide to her emotions: hence the rather extreme nature of the author's directions. On two successive pages we find the following notations for Maddy: *"the voice breaks . . . sobbing . . . Calmer . . . With anger . . . Sobbing . . . brokenly . . . exploding . . . She laughs wildly, ceases . . . Frenziedly . . . Faintly."* Since the audience can see Winnie as well as hear her, Beckett need not give his leading lady such emphatic stage directions.

Again, the difference in media has its effect on the physical image of the two women. Maddy says of herself,

> Oh I am just a hysterical old hag I know, destroyed with sorrow and pining and gentility and church-going and fat and rheumatism and childlessness.

Her husband describes her as "two hundred pounds of unhealthy fat." When Mr. Slocum is helping her into his car, she tells him to treat her "as if I were a bale, Mr. Slocum, don't be afraid," but this implies more cohesiveness than she in fact possesses — "heaving all over back and front." Winnie, on the other hand, is described in the stage directions as *"well preserved, blond for preference, plump, . . . big bosom. . . ."* There is nothing ridiculous or grotesque about her appearance, such as might deter a great lady of the theater from taking the part. Winnie's being buried to the waist in sand takes the place of all Maddy Rooney's painful or ridiculous disabilities — except that Winnie also suffers the handicap of short sight.

A closer reading of the plays shows that the two women have similar social, cultural and religious backgrounds. Maddy may seem the more *déclassée* of the two, but she is treated as a lady by everyone she meets. She uses the English language with care and precision, even though her command of archaic words and phrases justifies her husband's comment: "Do you know, Maddy, sometimes one would think you were struggling with a dead language." She only once quotes poetry ("Sigh out a something something tale of things, Done long ago and ill done"), but she is in the habit of reading a novel to Mr. Rooney — is it Krapp's favorite, *Effi Briest*, again? At least once in her life, she attended a lecture on psychoanalysis. As for religious observance, she is a faithful member of the Church of Ireland, who only last Sunday received communion in both kinds at her parish church and intends to hear tomorrow's sermon on the text "The Lord upholdeth all that fall and raiseth up all those that be bowed down."

It may seem ridiculous to speak of Winnie, symbolically posed in a purgatorial or hellish landscape, as having social, cultural and religious antecedents — yet these are all specifically referred to. In the opening moments of the play, for instance, we see her pray inaudibly, but she ends each of her two prayers with an audible Anglican formula: "For Jesus Christ sake Amen" and "World without end Amen." A few pages farther on, she remembers her first ball — and, quite oblivious of a possible double meaning, her second ball. These memories are enough in themselves to establish at least a middle-class social origin for her; that she remembers sitting on the knees of a future bishop is more equivocal evidence. As for her culture, quite early on she tries to remember Ophelia's "O! woe is me, / To have seen what I have seen, see what I see!" Soon afterwards, she uses the phrase "holy light," quoting *Paradise Lost*, and as she puts on her lipstick she subtly alludes to the last act of *Romeo and Juliet* with "Ensign crimson" and "Pale flag." I would describe her as a daughter of the Anglo-Irish gentry who has spent the approved number of years at a good Church of Ireland boarding-school. Her emotions and her speech, even when she believes she is unobserved by Willie, are more restrained than Maddy's. She examines Willie's dirty postcard closely, but her verdict on it — "Make any nice-minded person want to vomit" — implies that she herself is such a person: not too nice-minded, however, not to laugh at Willie's pun, "Formication."

Winnie's relationship with Willie is far more complex than that of Maddy with Mr. Rooney. Maddy is an example of truly dog-like devotion. Having only just recovered from a long illness, she struggles in infinite discomfort as far as the railway station to give her husband a surprise for his birthday by meeting his train. She suffers intense anxiety because the train is fifteen minutes late, but when the blind Mr. Rooney arrives, he is far from pleased by her surprise, because she has forgotten to "cancel the boy" who usually leads him home, and he must pay him a penny. Like a dog, Mrs. Rooney pleads for kindness: "Be nice to me, Dan, be nice to me today!" or "Put your arm round me." He grudgingly does so, but there is little evidence that their marriage has ever given her any greater satisfaction. As she has earlier said to Mr. Tyler, making a significant slip of the tongue over his name, "No, Mr. Rooney, Mr. Tyler I mean, I am tired of light old hands on my shoulders and other senseless places, sick and tired of them." Mr. Rooney himself says to her:

> Well! Did you ever know me to be well? The day you met me I should have been in bed. The day you proposed to me the doctors gave me up. You knew that, did you not? The night you married me they came for me with an ambulance. You have not forgotten that, I suppose?

One wonders why she ever married him: "Love, that is all I asked, a little love, daily, twice daily, fifty years of twice daily love like a Paris horse-butcher's regular, what normal woman wants affection?" If she asks urgently enough, Dan Rooney will put his arm round her, and even hold her tighter; he utters an occasional pitying phrase like "Poor Maddy!" Apart from that, she seems to get little of either love or affection. Rooney speaks of "the horrors of home life," and even of "the abhorred name" of his local station. The warmest image of domesticity he manages to conjure up is this: "Let us hasten home and sit before the fire. We shall draw the blinds. You will read to me. I think Effie is going to commit adultery with the Major." The rest of the time he treats her with anger or contempt because she cannot control her emotions: "Have you been drinking again? . . . You are quivering like a blanc-mange. . . . Pull yourself together. . . ." Yet she has her moment of happiness, of anticipation and even enjoyment:

> We shall hang up all our things in the hot-cupboard and get into our dressing-gowns. (*Pause.*) Put your arm

round me. (*Pause.*) Be nice to me! (*Pause. Gratefully.*)
Ah Dan!

A few minutes later, she learns why Dan's train was de-
layed: a little child fell out of the carriage under the wheels.
She must remember that earlier Dan has asked her, "Did
you ever wish to kill a child?" Whether or not he is himself
the cause of the child's death, the news of it surely puts an
end to all hope of further happiness for Maddy that day.

Willie of *Happy Days* is also a cross that his wife must
bear, but Winnie's attitude to him is that of a mother to
her naughty son rather than that of a dog to his master.
The first time that the audience hears his name is when
Winnie, with a tender smile, says "Poor Willie"; a little
later, she calls him "poor dear Willie." She pities him because he has "no zest . . . for anything . . . no interest
. . . in life" but envies his ability to "sleep for ever." Po-
litely but a little brusquely, she says, "Don't go off on me
again now dear will you please, I may need you." When he
is fully awake, she urges him to "slip on your drawers, dear,
before you get singed." Maternal solicitude is her com-
monest vein, varied by maternal reproof. Yet she in her turn
needs Willie: it makes her happy just to see him there, with
or without his drawers; it gives her a feeling of usefulness,
and even of power, when he responds to her requests, suggestions, or downright commands. Above all, she needs him
as an audience, a consciousness for whom she exists:

> Ah yes, if only I could bear to be alone, I mean prattle
> away with not a soul to hear. (*Pause.*) Not that I flatter
> myself you hear much, no Willie, God forbid. (*Pause.*)
> Days perhaps when you hear nothing. (*Pause.*) But days
> too when you answer. (*Pause.*) So that I may say at all

times, even when you do not answer and perhaps hear nothing, something of this is being heard, I am not merely talking to myself, that is in the wilderness, a thing I could never bear to do — for any length of time. (*Pause.*) That is what enables me to go on, go on talking that is. (*Pause.*) Whereas if you were to die — (*smile*) — to speak in the old style — (*smile off*) — or go away and leave me, then what would I do, what *could* I do, all day long, I mean between the bell for waking and the bell for sleep? (*Pause.*) Simply gaze before me with compressed lips. (*Long pause while she does so. . . .*) Not another word as long as I drew breath, nothing to break the silence of this place.

This is the longest, fullest statement in the play of a recurring idea of Winnie's. But if she needs Willie as an audience, it does not follow that he enjoys his appointed role. Only once does Winnie have serious misgivings on this point:

Oh I can well imagine what is passing through your mind, it is not enough to have to listen to the woman, now I must look at her as well. . . . Well it is very understandable. . . . Most understandable. . . . One does not appear to be asking a great deal, indeed at times it would seem hardly possible — (*voice breaks, falls to a murmur*) — to ask less — of a fellow-creature — to put it mildly — whereas actually — when you think about it — look into your heart — see the other — what he needs — peace — to be left in peace — then perhaps the moon — all this time — asking for the moon.

Perhaps peace is what Willie needs more than anything else. When he makes his final appearance at the end of Act II and gives Winnie the terrifying look that makes her wonder if he has gone mad, he may simply want to shut her up. Willie was always taciturn; as Winnie says, "Oh I know you were never one to talk, I worship you Winnie be mine and then nothing from that day forth only titbits from Reynolds' News." He has not given any sign of life for the entire second act, but since Winnie can no longer move her head, it is impossible for her to see whether he is still there or not. She calls him loudly but, when there is no answer, says, "Ah well, not to know, not to know for sure, great mercy, all I ask." When Willie, perhaps with murder in his heart, fails to reach up to her at the end of the play and murmurs, just audibly, the single syllable "Win," this is enough to fill her with happiness: she sings the refrain of the Waltz Song from *The Merry Widow*, which ends with the possibly ironic words, "It's true, it's true, / You love me so." At any rate, her dream has come true. Near the end of Act I, she said to Willie:

> Do you know what I dream sometimes? . . . That you'll come round and live this side where I could see you. . . . I'd be a different woman. . . . Unrecognizable. . . . Or just now and then, come round this side just every now and then and let me feast on you.

In the final stage direction, the feast seems to be over:

> *She turns her eyes, smiling, to* WILLIE, *still on his hands and knees looking up at her. Smile off. They look at each other. Long pause.*
> CURTAIN

Can this be the end of their relationship? At any rate, it has been one in which we can believe; extending over many years in the world we know and persisting, "to speak in the old style," beyond death. In Act I we saw them more or less

contented with their mutual boredom; in Act II, Willie
seems to have passed beyond that stage. Yet his present
dangerous mood may prove as temporary as others have
been. Looking at the revolver she has taken out of her bag,
Winnie reminds Willie of one such period:

> Remember how you used to keep on at me to take it
> away from you? Take it away, Winnie, take it away, be-
> fore I put myself out of my misery. (*Back front. De-
> risive.*) *Your* misery!

On the other hand, when Winnie catches sight of her parasol in Act II, an idyllic memory is evoked: "The sunshade
you gave me . . . that day . . . (*pause*) . . . that day
. . . the lake . . . the reeds." (The imagery reminds us of
Krapp's brief, unforgettable love scene.) In both acts Winnie nostalgically recalls her wedding day: "Golden you
called it [her hair], that day, when the last guest was
gone . . . ," and again, "That day. (*Pause.*) The pink
fizz. (*Pause.*) The flute glasses. (*Pause.*) The last guest
gone. (*Pause.*) The last bumper with the bodies nearly
touching. (*Pause.*) The look. (*Long pause.*)"

Their sexual relations do not seem to have been entirely
satisfactory, however, at least to Winnie:

> There was a time when I could have given you a hand.
> . . . And then a time before that again when I did give
> you a hand. . . . You were always in dire need of a
> hand, Willie.

As in *Krapp's Last Tape*, the conventionally idyllic is
undercut by ironic realism. Once again, in a relatively short
play, a whole life is evoked, but this time, instead of a
series of abortive relationships, a single sustained relation-

ship is recalled in all its happiness and misery. Thanks to Beckett's extraordinary power of compression, this very detailed account of an intense personal commitment is fitted in around what many critics have found even more absorbing — the account of Winnie's existential relationship with the universe. Winnie's meditations on the latter subject need not be examined here; I don't see that there is anything specifically feminine about them, except of necessity in the wording of a passage like this: "And should one day the earth cover my breasts, then I shall never have seen my breasts, no one ever seen my breasts." Winnie is conscious of her own subtlety and hopes that Willie has heard her philosophize: "I should be sorry to think you had caught nothing of all that, it is not every day I rise to such heights." Feminine or not, however, her reflections on time and being are at least the equal of any that Beckett has put in the mouths of his male characters.

As for *Not I*, while one could argue that Mouth's monologue is a logical development from Winnie's pseudo-dialogue, I think it can be much more plausibly viewed as a dramatization of *The Unnamable*. By putting "boy" for "girl" and changing the gender of the pronouns, *Not I* could become a monologue for male voice. Refusal to acknowledge responsibility for one's actions or to accept one's identity does not seem to be a peculiarly feminine trait. Technical considerations may have had more to do with the choice of sex: women do speak faster than men and scream more readily — at least according to the conventions of the English-speaking stage — while only a heavily made-up (and therefore feminine) mouth would be visible in the faint lighting Beckett calls for.

Enough, one of the late brief prose works, is narrated by a woman, though only the last sentence establishes the sex. In this character we recoguize almost the *reductio ad absurdum* of dog-like feminine devotion. Of her relationship as a child and adolescent with the old, bent man whom she met when she was no more than six, she says:

> I did all he desired. I desired it too. For him. Whenever he desired something so did I. He only had to say what thing. When he didn't desire anything neither did I. In this way I did not live without desires. If he had desired something for me I would have desired it too. Happiness for example or fame. I only had the desires he manifested. But he must have manifested them all. All his desires and needs. When he was silent he must have been like me. When he told me to lick his penis I hastened to do so. I drew satisfaction from it. We must have had the same satisfactions.
>
> One day he told me to leave him. It's the verb he used. He must have been on his last legs. I don't know if by that he meant me to leave him for good or only to step aside a moment. I never asked myself the question. I never asked myself any questions but his. Whatever it was he meant I made off without looking back. Gone from reach of his voice I was gone from his life. Perhaps it was that he desired. . . .

Since it is grouped among the "Residua" in *No's Knife*, *Enough* may be the surviving part of a longer work: the opening sentence, "All that goes before forget," tends to confirm this view. Nevertheless, this seven-page prose poem seems complete in itself, the last sentence deeply moving in its finality: "Enough my old breasts feel his old hand." As the narrator was still young when she left the old man, these eight words present an image of enduring emotion more vivid even than any in *Krapp's Last Tape*. In the piece as a whole Beckett's translation of his own French seems uncharacteristically clumsy, but the final sentence — perhaps because the adjective does not inflect in English — has a ring missing from the French: "Assez mes vieux seins sentent sa vieille main."

The longest piece of prose narrative that Beckett has written and published since *How It Is* is *The Lost Ones* (1972), translated from *Le Dépeupleur* (1970). Except for the opening sentence in each work, both French and English versions are written in what James Joyce once called "a style of scrupulous meanness." With mathematical pedantry it describes the dimensions, climate, and social arrangements of a cylinder containing "two hundred [naked] bodies in all round numbers. . . ." One may regard the cylinder as a microcosm of the human world or of Dante's *Inferno*, according to taste. In the opening sentence, however, it is described as "Abode where lost bodies roam each searching for its lost one." The corresponding sentence of the French original runs, "Séjour où des corps vont cherchant chacun son dépeupleur." According to Brian Finney, Beckett meant to refer the French reader to a famous line in the *Méditations poétiques* of the French Romantic poet Alphonse de Lamartine:[2]

Un seul être vous manque et tout est dépeuplé.

Translating the untranslatable, one produces something like the following: "You miss a single being and the whole world is unpeopled."

As might be expected from a work by Beckett, none of

the busy bodies in the cylinder ever does find its lost one. Gradually, first one and then another sinks down vanquished in the Belacqua position. Since the abode is circular and the wall, when seen from below, "presents an unbroken surface all the way round and up to the ceiling" — although in fact pierced by twenty niches — it is hard for those on the ground to orient themselves when they wish to climb up one of the fifteen ladders in order to search the niches.

> There does none the less exist a north in the guise of one of the vanquished or better one of the women vanquished or better still the woman vanquished [la vaincue]. She squats against the wall with her head between her knees and her legs in her arms. The left hand clasps the right shinbone and the right the left forearm. The red hair tarnished by the light hangs to the ground. It hides the face and whole front of the body down to the crutch. The left foot is crossed on the right. She is the north. She rather than some other among the vanquished because of her greater fixity. To one bent for once on taking his bearings she may be of help.

From time to time one of the searchers, thinking she may be the lost one, has examined her closely:

> The hair of the woman vanquished has thus many a time been gathered up and drawn back and the head raised and the face laid bare and whole front of the body down to the crutch. The inspection once completed it is usual to put everything carefully back in place as far as possible.

Having written the first fourteen paragraphs of Le Dépeupleur, Beckett, as he later told Finney, abandoned it "because of its complexity getting beyond control."[3] Then, immediately before its publication in 1970, Beckett added a fifteenth and final paragraph in which the last phase of the entropic process at work in the cylinder is imagined as having arrived:

> There he opens then his eyes this last of all if a man and some time later threads his way to that first among the vanquished so often taken for a guide. On his knees he parts the heavy hair and raises the unresisting head. Once devoured the face thus laid bare the eyes at a touch of the thumbs open without demur. In those calm wastes he lets his wander till they are the first to close and the head relinquished falls back into its place. He himself after a pause impossible to time finds at last his place and pose whereupon dark descends and at the same instant the temperature comes to rest not far from freezing point.

Has this man — if chance has made the last searcher in fact a man and not a woman — found his lost one? I doubt it, however full of Beckettian irony such an ending might be. What I want to stress, in any case, is the presence once more of that obsessive image, a woman's eyes that let a man enter and wander at will. To quote Krapp again:

> The eyes she had! . . . Everything there, everything on this old muckball, all the light and dark and famine and feasting of . . . the ages! (*In a shout.*) Yes! . . .

In the cruel world of *The Lost Ones*, fitfully agitated, ever changing, ever declining from worse to worse, one thing alone remains unchanged and undiminished — the calm beauty of a woman's eyes. It is no accident that the fixed north of that world is represented by the figure of a woman — drawn with fierce intensity by Avigdor Arikha in one of his illustrations for *The North*, an excerpt from *The Lost Ones* published in a limited edition. Fair to middling, good or bad, Beckett's women never change: their ardor for love and for suffering remains unquenchable to the gates of death and beyond.

EPILOGUE

Looking back on what I have written, I see now that, with a little rearrangement, all the oppositions which serve as nuclei for the preceding chapters can be roughly subsumed under one heading:

Intellect / Emotion

The World / Ireland
Gentleman / Tramp
Classicism / Absurdism
Painting / Music
Eye / Ear
Philosopher / Artist
Man / Woman

But "the danger is in the neatness of identifications" — to quote the opening sentence of Beckett's "Dante . . . Bruno . Vico . . Joyce." Painting and music, for example, are not true polar opposites: in fact, since one art is conditioned by space and the other by time, they are ultimately incommensurable. Yet literature, by appealing to Wordsworth's "inward eye" and the corresponding inward ear, can achieve a synthesis of space and time, of the visual and the aural. Furthermore, logic, biology and the politics of liberation all deny polarity between man and woman. My chapter headings can now be seen for what they are — a scaffolding. There remains the hope that when the scaffolding has been dismantled and taken away, a valid structure will be left standing: one that bears inspection from every side and can even be walked into and out of. The perfect critical description of an artist's achievement would resemble a crystal, revealing its own rightness by the symmetry and rationality of its form.

The imperfect structure that I have actually produced may suffer more from omissions than from any of its positive errors. For example, the equation of Ireland with emotion is hard to square with such facts as the following: Beckett's wife is French; Alfred Péron, once his closest friend, was French; it was for France that he chose to risk his life in the Resistance; it is in France that he chooses to live; it was in French that he first began "to write the things I feel." After the publication of Deirdre Bair's biography much will still remain to be discovered about the effect of life in France and of French culture generally upon Beckett as man and writer. Even to Beckett himself, the full extent of this influence must remain mysterious.

Another enemy of ideal perfection in the house of criticism is the fact that Mr. Beckett, I am happy to say, continues to write and publish in his seventy-first year. The latest works to reach the general public — as opposed to buyers of expensive limited editions — are the prose-poem *Still* (1974) and the short plays *Footfalls* and *That Time*, first performed at the Royal Court Theatre in the spring of 1976 as part of a series of plays honoring the author's seventieth birthday.

Still, mentioned in Chapter 5 because of Hayter's illustrations, describes in Beckett's late, telegraphic prose style a human figure sitting at a window to watch the sun go down. When night falls, the figure, "as if even in the dark eyes closed not enough . . . ," covers its eyes with a hand. The work ends with this sentence:

> Leave it so all quite still or try listening to the sounds all quite still head in hand listening for a sound.

The first chapter of *Murphy*, written nearly forty years earlier, ends in similar quietude, induced by the rapid movement of Murphy's rocking-chair:

> . . . the iridescence was gone, the cry in the mew was gone, soon his body would be quiet. Most things under the moon got slower and slower and then stopped, a rock got faster and faster and then stopped. Soon his body would be quiet, soon he would be free.

Footfalls, described on the cover as written specially for Billie Whitelaw, the London actress who created the part of Mouth in *Not I*, is another virtuoso exercise for one performer. The only visible character is May, who paces obsessively — seven steps one way, seven steps the other — across the bare stage. Presumably the Voice of May's unseen mother is a recording made by the actress who plays May;* for all we can tell, Voice may be a figment of May's imag-

* It could, however, be spoken live by another actress.

ination. Until the first blackout, there is dialogue between May, in her forties, and her bedridden mother, aged ninety: it culminates in the mother's question, "Will you never have done . . . revolving it all?" Between the first and second blackouts, only Voice speaks, while May stands still or paces. Voice tells the audience, "My voice is in her mind. . . . She fancies she is alone." Sometimes, we are told, May herself still speaks, "when she fancies none can hear. (*Pause.*) Tells how it was. (*Pause.*) Tries to tell how it was. (*Pause.*) It all. (*Pause.*) It all." After the second blackout, May alone speaks, relating a sequel in which an undefined "she," probably herself, has taken to haunting the local Anglican church, which she enters through a locked door; there she walks "up and down, up and down, his poor arm." We are not told whether this arm belongs to a dead father, brother, son, lover, or husband. Quite unexpectedly, "Old Mrs. Winter, whom the reader will remember," and her daughter Amy are mentioned. Mrs. Winter has become aware of something strange "at Evensong." As the play ends, Mrs. Winter is reported by May as speaking to Amy the very words spoken to May by her mother: "Will you never have done . . . revolving it all?"

Despite its insistence on favorite Beckett themes — woman's capacity for suffering and the axiom that the quantity of misery in the world always remains constant — *Footfalls* strikes me as somewhat bogus, the product of no stronger impulse than the playwright's fascination with the possibilities of his medium. *Krapp's Last Tape,* which also exploited a combination of live and recorded voices, used its new blend of stage and radio technique to make a profound new statement: not so *Footfalls*. *That Time*, on the other hand, while it can hardly be described as making a statement, uses a variation of the same technical means to create a unique mood.

The only visual element in *That Time* is the *"old white face"* of Listener, surrounded by *"long flaring white hair. . . . Voices ABC are his own coming to him from both sides and above."* Each voice deals with its own cluster of memories, but all must be recorded in such a way as to "relay one another without solution of continuity — apart from the two 10-second breaks." When the voices have been silent for three seconds during each of these breaks, Listener's eyes open, closing again after the words recommence. At the end of the play there is a third ten-second break before the curtain; after five seconds Listener produces a smile, *"toothless for preference."* Each third of the play consists of twelve speeches, four by each voice, arranged so that a different voice precedes every break. Listener is always addressed as "you," but the general effect is that of interior monologue.

Voice A, the most immediately Irish in rhythm and syntax, is concerned with "that time you went back that last time to look was the ruin still there where you hid as a child. . . ." According to this voice, Listener as a child sat on a stone inside the ruin and read all day or talked to himself, making up "imaginary conversations." Listener's older self, returning in search of his past, was supposedly frustrated by the disappearance of the number eleven tram — indeed of all trams — from his native city. As for the "Doric terminus of the Great Southern and Eastern," familiar from

Beckett's earlier work, it was "all closed down and boarded up." Dejected, Listener sat in a nearby doorway until it was time to catch the night ferry, never to return:

> making it all up on the doorstep as you went along making yourself all up again for the millionth time forgetting it all where you were and what for. . . .

Voice C similarly recalls or imagines a period in Listener's life when it was "always winter . . . always raining" and he used to take shelter in the Portrait Gallery or the Public Library or the Post Office:

> the rain and the old rounds trying making it up that way as you went along how it would work that way for a change never having been how never having been would work. . . .

In sharp contrast to these familiar predicaments, reminiscent of the trilogy and especially of *The Unnamable*, Voice B evokes a scene virtually without parallel in Beckett:

> on the stone together in the sun on the stone at the edge of the little wood and as far as eye could see the wheat turning yellow vowing every now and then you loved each other just a murmur not touching or anything of that nature you one end of the stone she the other. . . .

One finds nothing quite like this in *More Pricks than Kicks*, and the lovers in the punt of *Krapp's Last Tape* are probably much older and certainly less innocent; only the adolescent pair briefly seen holding hands in Part I of *How It Is* are at all comparable, but they are presented quite unsympathetically. No wonder Voice B says later, "hard to believe you even you made up that bit. . . ." Elsewhere, though, the same voice expresses utter skepticism:

> hard to believe harder and harder to believe you ever told anyone you loved them or anyone you till just one of those things you kept making up to keep the void out. . . .

Are they memories or fictions, these scenes evoked by the voices? Is all memory a fictional process, only slightly less deceptive in the average consciousness than it is in that of the artist? These Proustian questions are asked but not answered in *That Time*. All we can be sure of is that the child who sat on the stone in Foley's Folly, the young lover who sat on the stone by the wheat-field, the adult outcast who sank down on the marble bench in the Portrait Gallery, and the old man who drooled as he sat on a doorstep near the Doric terminus are aspects, real or imagined, of the same consciousness: Listener's, no doubt, but above all Beckett's own.

That Time ends with a smile from Listener which seems to be called forth by the last words of Voice C, "come and gone in no time gone in no time," suggesting that life, the voices, the play, or all three will soon be over. Seen in the perspective of eternity, Beckett's career as a writer may itself have come and gone in no time, but in purely human reckoning it has already lasted unusually long — nearly fifty years. For roughly half that time, from 1929 to the end of 1952, it was pursued in the face of almost total neglect. Despite Beckett's near-legendary modesty and distaste for publicity, not to mention the acute embarrassment he displayed on being awarded the Nobel Prize for Literature, it is therefore possible to argue that he is, quite unconsciously, an intensely ambitious man. As we have seen, his early literary criticism at once claimed total authority, especially when discussing writers as difficult as Joyce, Yeats or Proust. Similarly, his early poetry was as haughty as Pound's mature work in its refusal to explain itself; the notes to *Whoroscope* were only added at the publisher's request. The early fiction brooked no comparison with anyone of lesser stature than Joyce. For all the humility of the post-war writings, they displayed one classic piece of hubris — the ambition to use French as a Frenchman might. Repressed ambition has since come to the surface again disguised as perfectionism: the many drafts of a brief work like *Ping*, the obsessive attention to detail shown in stage directions and in the mounting of his own plays in Germany. I am prepared to argue that the brevity of the latter works is due not to any philosophical aspiration towards silence but to this perfectionism: the only perfectly finished piece of workmanship is the miniature.

Another paradox that becomes more evident as Beckett moves beyond the normal span of three score years and ten is that of the author who says life has nothing to commend it except brevity yet seems to cling to it fairly tenaciously. Nevertheless, my own severest criticism of Beckett's *œuvre* is based not on its pessimism but on its proneness to self-pity, even though that self-pity is of a very special kind, expressed by his characters on behalf of the human race. It is more than a joke when Didi and Gogo insist that their sufferings are greater than Christ's because "where he lived it was warm, it was dry! . . . Yes. And they crucified quick."* Beckett implicitly praises Murphy because he

* See above, p. 72.

does not "whinge"; neither does Winnie in *Happy Days*; most Beckett characters, however, bemoan their lot in the manner of Job but without the briskness of Neary, who "leaned against the Pillar railings and cursed, first the day in which he was born, then — in a bold flash-back — the night in which he was conceived." *Footfalls* provides yet another example of this nagging pity for the human condition that too closely resembles collective self-pity. When May asks her mother, "Would you like me to inject you again? . . . Dress your sores? . . . Sponge you down? . . . Moisten your poor lips? . . . Pray with you? . . . For you?" human suffering is again being compared with that of Christ. One is left wondering why so few of Beckett's characters carry their distaste for life to its logical conclusion in self-destruction: there seems to be a higher proportion of suicides in Dante's inferno than there is in Beckett's.

"I greatly fear," says Wylie at a certain point in *Murphy*, "that the syndrome known as life is too diffuse to admit of palliation. For every symptom that is eased, another is made worse." Thirty-eight years after first reading those discouraging words, I find Beckett still conveying the same message in *Footfalls* and, with greater subtlety, in *That Time*, where we can accept that symptoms are really eased for a time by love and not merely by injections.

Yet Wylie was wrong, even for those who grudgingly or gleefully accept his estimate of life at face value. One palliation at least is granted us, the heightened awareness of life that is communicated through the artist's vision. Perhaps that is the true secret behind Listener's smile.

NOTES

1 THESIS / ANTITHESIS

1. Oscar Wilde, "The Truth of Masks," *Intentions* (London: Osgood, McIlvaine & Co., 1894), p. 258.
2. W. B. Yeats, "Per Amica Silentia Lunae," *Mythologies* (London: Macmillan, 1959), p. 328.
3. Andrew Belis (pseudonym of Samuel Beckett), "Recent Irish Poetry," *Bookman*, 86 (August 1934): 235.
4. W. B. Yeats, "Coole Park and Ballylee, 1931," *Collected Poems*, 2nd ed. (London: Macmillan, 1950), p. 276.
5. John Gruen, "Samuel Beckett Talks About Beckett," *Vogue*, London ed. (February 1970), p. 108.
6. Israel Shenker, "Moody Man of Letters," *New York Times*, 6 May 1956, sec. 2, pp. 1, 3.
7. James Knowlson, *Light and Darkness in the Theatre of Samuel Beckett* (London: Turret Books, 1972), p. 40.
8. Knowlson, p. 47.
9. Shenker, p. 3.
10. Brian Finney, *"Since How It Is": A Study of Samuel Beckett's Later Fiction* (London: Covent Garden Press, 1972), p. 10.
11. Finney, p. 9.
12. David H. Hesla, *The Shape of Chaos: An Interpretation of the Art of Samuel Beckett* (Minneapolis: University of Minnesota Press, 1971), p. 215.

239

13. Hesla, p. 216.
14. Quoted in Alec Reid, *All I Can Manage, More Than I Could*, 2nd ed. (Dublin: Dolmen Press, 1969), p. 11.
15. Finney, pp. 39-40.
16. "Recent Irish Poetry," p. 235.

2   IRELAND / THE WORLD

1. This quotation is taken from an announcement that the house was for sale by public auction on 20 November 1975. Along with other possible buyers, I visited "Cooldrinagh" a few days before the sale and noted the bell indicator then.
2. Vivian Mercier, *The Irish Comic Tradition* (Oxford: Clarendon Press, 1962), pp. 75-76.
3. James Knowlson, *Samuel Beckett: An Exhibition* (London: Turret Books, 1971), p. 23.
4. Knowlson, p. 23.
5. Quoted in Knowlson, pp. 22-23.
6. W. B. Yeats, *Collected Plays*, 2nd ed. (London: Macmillan, 1952), p. 693.
7. Conversation with Francis Warner.
8. Jack B. Yeats, *Collected Plays*, ed. Robin Skelton (London: Secker & Warburg, 1971), p. 9.
9. Vivian Mercier, "Beckett and the Search for Self," *New Republic*, 133 (19 September 1955): 20.
10. Martin Esslin, "Samuel Beckett: The Search for the Self," *The Theatre of the Absurd*, rev. ed. (Harmondsworth, Eng.: Penguin Books, 1968), pp. 29-30.
11. A remarkably full picture of the social and economic level of the residents of the Foxrock Estate during the years 1903-50, when members of the Beckett family lived there, can be gathered from the annual volumes of *Thom's Dublin Directory*.
12. John Hewitt, "No Rootless Colonist," *Aquarius* (Benburb, N. Ireland), no. 5 (1972), p. 90.
13. Hewitt, p. 93.
14. Hewitt, p. 93.
15. Lawrence E. Harvey, *Samuel Beckett: Poet and Critic* (Princeton, N.J.: Princeton University Press, 1970), p. 67.
16. Here and elsewhere I have referred often to the "Chronology of Beckett's Life" in Ruby Cohn, *Back to Beckett* (Princeton,

N.J.: Princeton University Press, 1973), pp. vii-xii. I have also drawn on my own acquaintance with Beckett and Dublin and on the researches of Deirdre Bair.

17. *Trinity College Record Volume* (Dublin: Hodges, Figgis & Co., 1951), pp. 99, 282, 340, 357, 363.
18. Conversation with Professor Maguinness, London, September 1975.
19. Gabriel d'Aubarède, "Waiting for Beckett," *Trace*, no. 42 (Summer 1961), p. 158. Translated by Christopher Waters from the original French in *Nouvelles Littéraires*, 16 February 1961.
20. Harvey, p. 415.
21. Andrew Belis (pseudonym of Samuel Beckett), "Recent Irish Poetry," *Bookman*, 86 (August 1934): 236.
22. Alec Reid, *All I Can Manage, More Than I Could*, 2nd ed. (Dublin: Dolmen Press, 1969), p. 68.
23. Marilyn Gaddis Rose, "The Irish Memories of Beckett's Voice," *Journal of Modern Literature*, 2 (September 1971): 127-32.
24. For a fuller discussion, see Vivian Mercier, "Beckett's Anglo-Irish Stage Dialects," *James Joyce Quarterly*, 8 (Beckett issue, Summer 1971): 311-17.
25. "Recent Irish Poetry," p. 235. See p. 100 of this book.

3   GENTLEMAN / TRAMP

1. See for example the illustration facing p. 109 in Ruby Cohn, *Back to Beckett* (Princeton, N.J.: Princeton University Press, 1973).
2. Letter from Beckett to Alan Schneider, dated 29 December 1957, in *Village Voice*, 19 March 1958, p. 15.
3. See the photograph of William Beckett in Ludovic Janvier, *Samuel Beckett par lui-même* (Paris: Seuil, 1969), p. [8].
4. Janvier, p. [17].
5. Reproduced facing p. 24 in *Beckett at 60: A Festschrift* (London: Calder & Boyars, 1967).
6. Raymond Federman and John Fletcher, *Samuel Beckett: His Works and His Critics* (Berkeley: University of California Press, 1970), p. 77.

4 CLASSICISM / ABSURDISM

1. Vivian Mercier, "The Uneventful Event," *Irish Times*, 18 February 1956.
2. Fowlie and Belmont are quoted in Raymond Federman and John Fletcher, *Samuel Beckett: His Works and His Critics* (Berkeley: University of California Press, 1970), pp. 170, 191.
3. Lucien Goldmann, *Racine*, tr. Alastair Hamilton (Cambridge: Rivers Press, 1972), p. 4. Italics in the original.
4. Goldmann, p. 5.
5. Goldmann, p. 32.
6. Alain Robbe-Grillet, *For a New Novel*, tr. Richard Howard (New York: Grove Press, 1965), pp. 120-21.

5 PAINTING / MUSIC

1. "La Peinture des Van Velde ou le monde et le pantalon," original typescript, p. 1. Translated by VM.
2. "MacGreevy on Yeats," original typescript, p. 1.
3. For most of the biographical material in this chapter and for the loan of photocopies I am deeply grateful to Deirdre Bair.
4. Hilary Pyle, *Jack B. Yeats* (London: Routledge & Kegan Paul, 1970), p. 146.
5. Information from Deirdre Bair.
6. Sources: (a) photocopy of original typescript, Dartmouth College, 3 pp.; (b) photocopy of original typescript, Dartmouth College, 11 pp.; (c) photocopy from *Derrière le miroir*, nos. 11-12 (June 1948), pp. 3-4, 7; (d) *Proust and Three Dialogues* (London: Calder & Boyars, 1970), pp. 94-126; (e) *Lettres Nouvelles*, 2 (April 1954): 619-20; (f) photocopy from *Henri Hayden: Recent Paintings* (catalogue of an exhibition at the Waddington Galleries, London, 12 February–7 March 1959), p. [2].
7. "Denis Devlin," reprinted in *Lace Curtain*, no. 3 (Summer 1970), pp. 41-44.
8. Information from the Hayter exhibition at the Neptune Gallery, Dublin, 13 June–19 July 1975, and from its catalogue. For a readily accessible text of *Still*, see Samuel Beckett and Others, *Signature Anthology* (London: Calder & Boyars, 1975), pp. 13-16.

9. *Derrière le miroir*, nos. 11-12 (June 1948), p. 4. Translated by VM.

10. Andrew Belis (pseudonym of Samuel Beckett), "Recent Irish Poetry," *Bookman*, 86 (August 1934): 235.

11. Lawrence E. Harvey, *Samuel Beckett: Poet and Critic* (Princeton, N.J.: Princeton University Press, 1970), p. 424n. On pp. 419-41 Harvey discusses Beckett's art criticism more fully than any previous writer had done, using it as a guide to Beckett's literary aesthetic; he is not, however, interested in its value as a guide to Beckett's knowledge of contemporary painters other than the Van Veldes and Jack Yeats.

12. "La Peinture des Van Velde," typescript, p. 7. Translated by VM.

13. "La Peinture des Van Velde," p. 8.

14. This extract and the four following ones are from "Peintres de l'empêchement," translated by VM. No page references are given, since the article contains only three pages.

15. Many of Beckett's protagonists have reminded critics, myself included, of the clown-Christs and Christ-clowns painted by Rouault. This passage confirms one's guess that Beckett knows and admires these compelling images.

16. This refers to a passage I have not quoted, in which Beckett asks, "How would it be if I first said what I am pleased to fancy he [Bram van Velde] is, fancy he does, and then that it is more than likely that he is and does quite otherwise?" Duthuit answers, "Do as you please."

17. This and the other passages quoted from Beckett's one-page appreciation are translated, with misgivings, by VM.

18. "La Peinture des Van Velde," typescript, p. 1.

19. Eugene Webb, *The Plays of Samuel Beckett* (Seattle: University of Washington Press, 1972), pp. 43-44, 51, 95-96, 102-4, 113-15. Eugene Webb, *Samuel Beckett: A Study of His Novels* (Seattle & London: University of Washington Press, 1973), pp. 154, 162-68.

20. The late Dr. J. A. Wallace of Dublin to Deirdre Bair.

6 EYE / EAR

1. See Appendix II in Raymond Federman and John Fletcher, *Samuel Beckett: His Works and His Critics* (Berkeley: University of California Press, 1970), pp. 325-43.
2. Alan Schneider, "On Directing *Film*," in Samuel Beckett, *Film* (London: Faber & Faber, 1972), pp. 85, 88. For photographs of the eye, see p. 9 of *Film*.
3. Letter to George Reavey, 27 September 1938. Information supplied by Deirdre Bair.
4. Hugh Kenner, *Samuel Beckett: A Critical Study*, 2nd ed. (Berkeley: University of California Press, 1968), p. 91.
5. Federman and Fletcher, p. 82.
6. Marcel Mihalovici, "My Collaboration with Samuel Beckett," in *Beckett at 60: A Festschrift* (London: Calder & Boyars, 1967), p. 21. For further information about the opera, see Federman and Fletcher, pp. 41-42.
7. Mihalovici, pp. 20-21.
8. "Un Collaborateur: Marcel Mihalovici," in Pierre Mélèse, *Samuel Beckett* (Paris: Seghers, 1966), p. 155. Translated by VM.
9. Mélèse, p. 155.
10. Samuel Beckett, *Proust and Three Dialogues* (London: Calder & Boyars, 1970), p. 92.
11. *Proust*, p. 74.

7 ARTIST / PHILOSOPHER

1. Gabriel d'Aubarède, "Waiting for Beckett," *Trace*, no. 42 (Summer 1961), p. 157. Translated by Christopher Waters from the original French in *Nouvelles Littéraires*, 16 February 1961.
2. Jean Onimus, *Beckett* (Paris and Bruges: Desclée de Brouwer, 1968), p. 24. This contribution to the series *Les Ecrivains devant Dieu* is in my opinion the best study of Beckett from a Christian standpoint yet published in either French or English.
3. David H. Hesla, *The Shape of Chaos: An Interpretation of the Art of Samuel Beckett* (Minneapolis: University of Minnesota Press, 1971), p. 15.

4. Quoted by Alan Schneider, "Waiting for Beckett," in *Beckett at 60: A Festschrift* (London: Calder & Boyars, 1967), p. 34.
5. Samuel Beckett and Others, *Our Exagmination Round His Factification for Incamination of Work in Progress* (London: Faber & Faber, 1972), p. 7.
6. See Vivian H. S. Mercier, "*Tristram Shandy* and Locke's *Essay Concerning Human Understanding*," *Dublin Magazine*, n.s., 18 (October–December 1943): 32-37.
7. Blaise Pascal, *Pensées*, tr. A. J. Krailsheimer (Harmondsworth, Eng.: Penguin Books, 1966), pp. 58-59. (Brunschvicg ed. no. 339.)
8. Pascal, pp. 67, 235. (Brunschvicg ed. nos. 139, 131.)
9. *Village Voice*, 19 March 1958, p. 8.
10. *Our Exagmination*, pp. 21, 22.

8 WOMAN / MAN

1. *Village Voice*, 19 March 1958, p. 8.
2. Brian Finney, "*Since How It Is*": A Study of Samuel Beckett's *Later Fiction* (London: Covent Garden Press, 1972), p. 11.
3. Finney, p. 9.

INDEX

All titles given in italics or within quotation marks refer to individual works by Samuel Beckett, collections of his work, or collections in which a work of his appears; the few exceptions are indicated. The names of other authors are listed but not the titles of their works.